Writing to Develop
Mathematical Understanding

Writing to Develop
Mathematical Understanding

David K. Pugalee
University of North Carolina Charlotte

Christopher-Gordon Publishers, Inc.
Norwood, Massachusetts

Copyright Acknowledgments

Christopher~Gordon Publishers, Inc.
Bridging Theory and Practice

1502 Providence Highway, Suite #12
Norwood, Massachusetts 02062
800-934-8322
781-762-5577
www.Christopher-Gordon.com

Printed in the United State of America
10 9 8 7 6 5 4 3 2 1   09 08 07 06

ISBN: 1-929024-86-X
Library of Congress Catalogue Number: 2005924176

Contents

Introduction

Writing in mathematics? As suspect as it might sound, writing is an important learning tool that has the potential to promote students' understanding of mathematics. Despite the popularity of the writing across the curriculum movement that began in the late 1970s, writing has not been widely emphasized in the teaching of mathematics. Recognition of the link between thinking and writing, as well as the influence of national standards that emphasize communication in mathematics, has contributed to a recent interest in the connection between writing and mathematics. This book will explore that relationship and provide practical information to guide planning, implementing, and evaluating writing in the mathematics classroom. The ideas presented in this work promote the idea that writing can be a powerful tool in developing students' mathematical literacy.

Mathematical literacy is characterized by a conceptual level of mathematical understanding.[1] The primary goal of a curriculum that promotes mathematical literacy is to develop students who can reason mathematically. Writing promotes this level of mathematical reasoning by providing a mechanism by which students can think about and verbalize important mathematical concepts and ideas. Through these processes, students gain ownership of essential mathematical concepts that provide a basis for ongoing growth of mathematical skills and understanding.

The Writing and Thinking Connection

The writing and thinking connection has long been discussed in circles outside mathematics. Lev Vygotsky (1987), a Russian psychologist whose writings have greatly influenced current educational practices, saw writing as requiring deliberate analytical action on the part of the person doing the composing. He also saw writing as requiring a deliberate structure of a web of meaning as the writer formed associations between current and new knowledge.

Those who have studied writing and composing attest that writing is a generative act that helps students to analyze, compare facts, and synthesize information (Farrell, 1978). Others see writing and problem solving as intricately linked processes involving stages of planning, executing, and evaluating—comparable processes in both writing and problem solving (Flower & Hayes, 1983). The connection between writing and problem solving is important because writing activities that promote learning must go beyond reproducing information. Boscolo and Mason (2001) summarize these ideas in saying that "writing can improve students' learning by promoting active knowledge construction that requires them to be involved in transforming rather than a process of reproducing" (p. 85). As students write, they manipulate, integrate, and restructure knowledge through using and reflecting on what they know and believe. This process facilitates the development of meaningful understanding: The more a student works with ideas and concepts, the more likely those ideas and concepts will be understood and remembered.

The following benefits are derived from writing:

- Students are engaged in active learning.
- Students acquire ownership by using their own language to express concepts.
- Students have an opportunity to write to multiple audiences, such as teachers and peers.
- Students can reflect on what they know or are learning.
- Students discover what they don't know or are having difficulty understanding.
- Activities can be adapted for individual, small-group, or whole-class instruction.
- Writing allows for formative as well as summative assessment.
- Writing creates opportunities for dialogue and discussion.

Connecting Writing to Learning Mathematics

Communication is an important process skill for learning mathematics. It is so important that it is identified as one of five process skills by the National Council of Teachers of Mathematics (2000) in its standards document, along with problem solving, reasoning and proof, connections, and representation. These standards identify four goals related to communication for mathematics students in prekindergarten through grade 12.[2] These goals are as follows:

- Organize and consolidate mathematical thinking through communication
- Communicate mathematical thinking coherently and clearly to peers, teachers, and others
- Analyze and evaluate the mathematical thinking and strategies of others
- Use the language of mathematics to express mathematical ideas precisely

Although this document includes oral and written expression in the communication goal, there is a specific emphasis on the importance of writing in promoting students' mathematical literacy. Writing is seen as a tool for helping students to consolidate their thinking as they reflect on their work and justify their thoughts. These goals for communication will be revisited as we develop specific ideas about using writing in the mathematics classroom.

Mathematical literacy should be the goal for all mathematics programs. While mathematical literacy includes content knowledge that prepares students to function in society, there are also process skills that are central to an individual's capacity for doing and understanding mathematics. Communication, including written forms, is part of this dynamic interplay between content and process. In the model of mathematical literacy shown in Figure I-1, the outer circle contains the processes that are important in helping students to develop a conceptual understanding of mathematics. The inner circle contains the "enablers," or those tools that facilitate the doing of mathematics (Pugalee, 1999).

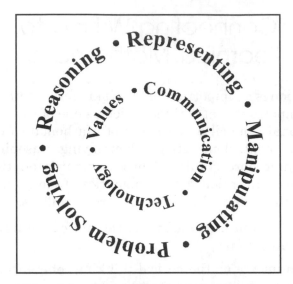

Figure I-1.   Model of Mathematical Literacy

This model shows how essential communication is in developing students' capacity to reason and think mathematically. Written communication is a vital element in promoting the level of learning that helps students to attain mathematical literacy. Research on writing and mathematics supports the premise that writing supports deeper mathematical understanding through an emphasis on students' critical thinking.[3] In fact, writing has been shown to support the development of metacognition, which is sometimes thought of as thinking about thinking and includes those thinking skills that help students to monitor their thinking processes (Artz & Armour-Thomas, 1992; Carr & Biddlecomb, 1998; Powell, 1997; Pugalee, 2001a, 2003). These studies show how writing provides a level of reflection and analysis that helps students to focus on their thinking about the mathematical processes in which they are engaged. It is through this reflection and analysis that students' thought processes become visible through the written word. This visibility is most powerful for the student who makes connections between significant mathematical concepts and ideas as well as for the audience for whom the writing is intended.

> Mathematics is no different from the rest of experience; it is a topic which we store in our heads as a narrative—a story about what we know, what we don't know, and what we wish to know. It's a story we must share with other people to see if we've got it right, to fill in the gaps, to make it grow. (Meier & Rishel, 1998, p. xi)

Writing can be an amazing learning tool for mathematics; however, most teachers have little experience with writing in mathematics. Many elementary teachers include some form of writing in mathematics, but in general such practices may be isolated and viewed as extras. In the traditional mathematics instruction paradigm, the teacher presents information and how-to, and the students practice. There are few or no opportunities for students to verbalize the concepts and ideas presented to them. Given that language is the basis of learning, students need opportunities to verbalize the mathematics that they are encountering. There are many issues to consider. In order for writing in mathematics to produce the kind of learning outcomes that make it a viable instructional strategy, it must be carefully planned, implemented, and evaluated. This book is about those issues. The material presented will provide a guide for transforming mathematics instruction through the use of writing as a tool for learning.

Organization of the Book

This book is organized into four sections, three main sections and a follow-up. Each of the first three sections corresponds to one of the phases of effective instructional design: planning, implementing, and assessing.[4] Each of these phases might be thought of in terms of an overarching question that guides the process.

Planning. How do I design writing activities and exercises that help students meaningfully understand the mathematics being taught? This section will include a discussion of how mathematics teachers, who might have little training in teaching writing, can develop students' writing skills within the context of teaching mathematics. A sound process for developing meaningful activities and exercises will be the focus of another chapter. These principles will be brought together in some ideas about planning instruction in which communication and mathematics are intertwined in the process of learning.

Implementing. How do I effectively use writing as part of instruction so that it is effective, efficient, and engaging? This section will address key issues about what happens when writing is used in mathematics instruction. How does a teacher develop clear expectations and help students to understand the importance of writing in learning mathematics? Included are effective strategies and methods for using writing in the mathematics classroom, with an emphasis on how to focus on the key mathematical ideas and concepts being taught.

Assessing. How do I use writing to evaluate the mathematical knowledge and understanding of students, in addition to their ability to communicate mathematically? Assessing the writing that students produce sometimes seems overwhelming for the mathematics teacher. This section will provide some guidelines and suggestions for managing students' writing. Assessment techniques and strategies will be presented, including the development of rubrics and the use of peer evaluation. Writing provides rich evidence of student learning. This section will discuss some ways to make this process feasible and successful.

Following up. Once writing is an integral part of mathematics instruction, how can this process be strengthened? This section will discuss how writing extends students' mathematical understanding, with an emphasis on developing metacognitive skills. Some strategies for challenging and extending students' reasoning through writing will be presented. A final chapter will discuss how professional networks can help to support writing and mathematical connections. Resource ideas to support the use of writing in mathematics will be offered. Some suggestions on what can be done in the school and beyond to promote writing as an integral part of mathematics will also be discussed.

Notes

1. Mathematical literacy, like literacy in general, is difficult to define. The definition offered here avoids specifying skills and content knowledge, but it recognizes that these are very important. Mathematical literacy is best viewed as a set of thinking processes that has certain characteristics. One such model is offered in Pugalee (1999) and is presented in this section.

2. The NCTM standards include five content strands and five process strands. The five content strands are number and operations, algebra, geometry, measurement, and data analysis and probability. For each of these strands, the standards document gives common goals for all students in pre-K through grade 12, but it offers differentiated expectations for each of the grade-level bands: pre-K through 2, grades 3 through 5, grades 6 through 8, and grades 9 through 12. The process strands, which include communication, give common goals for students in pre-K through 12. There are no differentiated expectations for the grade-level bands, but the document does provide some description of what these process standards should look like at the various grade-level bands.

3. Morgan (1998, pp. 26–28) summarizes some of the cognitive gains reported in the literature, including writing in mathematics for problem solving, applications, summaries of work done, responses to writing prompts, writing word problems, writing about solutions, writing definitions, and translating other representations into words.

4. Most instructional design models include three phases: planning, implementing, and evaluating or assessing. These three phases provide a framework for organizing important ideas and strategies that support the effective use of writing in the mathematics classroom.

Planning

Chapter

1

Planning for Instruction That Develops Written Communication Skills

Developing Written Communication Skills: Some Basic Ideas

Writing is an integral part of the study of any content area; however, mathematics may be the subject least likely to emphasize the development of such skills. Although teaching mathematical content is the primary responsibility of the mathematics teachers, the teacher can positively impact the development of writing skills without compromising on the mathematics that must be taught. We want students to have the ability to reason mathematically, and writing can help to facilitate learning mathematics. Thus, in the long run, writing and mathematics have a wonderfully mutual relationship, in which writing becomes one of the tools that the teacher can use to develop mathematical understanding.[1]

Moffet's (1981) model of coding clearly illustrates how writing supports the attainment of mathematical literacy, the ability of students to use mathematical concepts and ideas to reason about mathematical situations and solve problems. Moffet's model begins with nonverbal levels where experience is coded into concepts—that is, concept formation. Next, these ideas are put into speech; this is the oral level. Vygotsky (1987) wrote about "inner speech" and verbal thinking as a complex dynamic between thought and word. Thus, the last level is that of the written word, where speech is put into print. This last level is considered the written level of literacy. The act of writing is generative, involving the organization, reflection, and revision of thinking. This movement, from conceptualization to verbalization to literacy, makes it clear that an emphasis on language must be a significant part of mathematics instruction if students are to really understand the mathematics that they encounter.[2] Writing is a means of externalizing these thinking processes—a conceptualization and synthesis of the reasoning and thinking that engages students in the mathematics they experience. Table 1-1 shows these levels of coding.

Table 1-1. Levels of Coding

Experience into Thought	*Nonverbal*	*Conceptualization*
Thought into Speech	*Oral*	*Verbalization*
Speech into Print	*Written*	*Literacy*

The teacher creates an environment that supports the use of a writing-to-learn framework. This environment is influenced by how writing is treated in the mathematics classroom. Students should view writing as an integral part of their mathematics instruction. Tynjala, Mason, & Lonka (2001) indicate that students' conceptions of learning are related to how they view the aim of such writing tasks. As such, writing in mathematics should promote an active engagement of students in written work that is viewed as related to knowledge instead of related to recounting and stating information. While recounting and stating information has its place as a purpose of writing, this form of writing should not dominate the types of writing in which students are asked to engage. In a positive environment, students will "own" the writing that they produce and will "own" the mathematical ideas and concepts that they give voice to through their written words. The focus of this chapter is to provide the mathematics teacher with a framework for thinking about writing in mathematics. This framework, consisting of five principles that are used across the curriculum, provides a critical lens that impacts the instructional planning process and the way that writing is conceptualized and viewed as part of the trajectory for learning mathematics. It isn't reasonable to expect mathematics teachers to be experts on teaching writing, but there are some basic principles that can be easily reinforced in the mathematics classroom.

Principle 1:
The Writing Process Has Three Phases

Teachers of mathematics can reinforce the writing process, which consists of planning, composing, and revising. These main phases provide a basis for helping students to view writing as a process for learning. There are other approaches to writing that include more phases, but these three main phases provide an accessible model for teachers who may not have formalized training in teaching writing. These phases have been instrumental in shaping writing research (Hayes & Flower, 1980). Planning involves the acquisition of information, organization of those ideas, and setting goals related to the identified task. Composing involves the creation of written texts to express the ideas identified during the planning phase. Revising involves the writer in considering the quality of the written product and evaluating the degree to which the text meets the criteria of the task. Mathematics teachers will recognize that these processes provide not only a framework for writing but also an approach for any learning task. Such behaviors are not inherently different from the mathematical problem-solving phases of orientation, organization, execution, and verification (Figure 1-1). It is important for students to see the parallel between the thinking processes used in writing and those in approaching a mathematics problem. These are not additional thinking processes to develop, but known processes that need to be reinforced in a different setting. This is an important guiding principle that teachers should consider broadly when planning mathematics lessons. By being aware of these three processes, the teacher can consider appropriate ways to reinforce those processes when teaching mathematics. Such actions will serve to support a

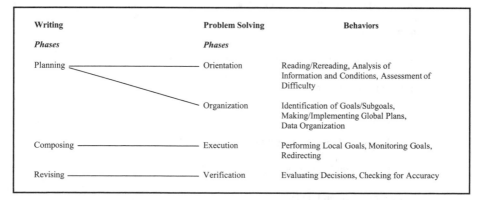

Figure 1-1. Comparison of Writing and Problem-Solving Processes

classroom environment in which writing is valued. Emphasizing these three processes is one of several important principles that are easily incorporated into mathematics classrooms, and it provides some general ideas for the teacher to consider as plans are made for effective, efficient, and engaging mathematics teaching.

Let's consider the three phases of the writing process and apply them to the teaching and learning of mathematics. This will help us to develop some overarching ideas to be considered in planning mathematics instruction. An important component of planning instruction is to identify goals and to identify what it is that students should learn. The following ideas show how writing can be supported in planning mathematics instruction through a lens that takes the three writing phases into consideration. This approach has to be two-pronged: The focus has to include broad processes that students should learn as well as teaching principles that support students in developing those processes. For each phase, let's consider overarching questions for the students and the teacher. The student questions will serve as general considerations that will help us to establish the learning goals for each of the three phases. The teacher questions will help us to facilitate the students' success with the task. Students might be given a copy of the student questions to guide them in writing assignments in mathematics as well as other content areas. A reproducible copy of the student questions for their use is included as Table 1-2.

Table 1-2.   Questions to Guide Students in Planning, Composing, and Revising Written Work

Planning
Do I understand what I am being asked?
Composing
What concepts and ideas support the statements I am making?
How can I describe my thinking concisely and clearly?
Revising
Have I answered the question fully?
Are my conjectures and ideas supported?
Is my work clear and understandable?

Planning

Student Question: Do I understand what I am being asked?

Teacher Question: Are my writing assignments stated clearly and are the expectations communicated?

Planning involves some initial consideration of the task, with the students assessing whether they understand what the task is asking them to do. Although this seems obvious, many students have not developed habits of mind whereby they routinely reflect on the nature of an assignment and assess whether they understand what their goal should be in completing the task. This type of thinking clearly parallels student behaviors that are good for doing mathematics, particularly solving problems. Students must understand what a problem or task is asking before they can successfully proceed. In writing, students must understand what they are to address in order to meet the goal(s) of the writing task. Tasks and assignments should be clearly stated so that students understand what they are being asked to do. Students should understand the mathematical nature of the writing task as well as the level and/or type of writing that the teacher expects. Initially, the level of specificity for the types of writing that should be produced and the expected content will be high. Once students develop some ideas about the types of assignments and their purposes, they will be able to make judgments about the level of writing required and the format that such writing should take.

The teacher facilitates the students' planning behaviors. Clearly stated information and directions for writing tasks and understood expectations are key at this stage. Tasks that are authentic[3] and open-ended allow students to demonstrate their understanding and make conceptual connections; however, the directions and information related to those tasks must contain enough structure so that the students' writing provides meaningful information related to the mathematics being considered. We will consider how students internalize expectations with greater detail in chapters 4 through 6 when we discuss implementation issues. When the teacher is planning for writing tasks, key words and phrases help to communicate clear expectations for the assignments. The information below in Table 1-3 considers some language that will help to make the tasks clear. The key terms are not exhaustive but will provide some structure for helping the teacher to construct clear tasks.

Table 1-3.   Key Terms for Clear Writing Tasks

Compare and/or Contrast
Write about what is different and/or what is alike.

Describe
Provide step-by-step details using key terms, graphs, charts, diagrams, and other illustrations. Make sure the illustrations and diagrams are referred to in the descriptions.

Explain
Elaborate on solutions, steps, ideas, concepts, and conjectures using numbers, symbols, illustrations, and examples when it helps to make your explanations clear.

Interpret
Provide mathematical reasoning to describe relationships (e.g., mathematical information contained in data tables or charts, graphs, illustrations, models, diagrams, symbolic representations, and other ways of representing information and interactions).

Provide Reasons or Justification
Give supporting evidence from mathematics to support your thinking, including examples, mathematical concepts and definitions, theorems, and other reasons that support what you say.

List
Provide ideas in a numbered or bulleted format.

Show All Work
Include all calculations, steps, and ideas that you thought about and used to reach your conclusion—all information that shows your thinking.

Composing

Student Questions: What concepts and ideas support the statements I am making? How can I describe my thinking concisely and clearly?

Teacher Questions: What is the important mathematical content that must be accessible to the student? How can the written content reflect good mathematical thinking? What strategies can be emphasized for organizing and communicating that information?

Composing is the most time-consuming of the three phases, requiring the writer to produce text that moves toward completing the understood goal of the task. Students focus on two important questions that revolve around the issue of information and how to communicate that information. Students access important mathematical concepts and ideas and construct various written statements that concisely and clearly communicate their ideas. As the teacher plans for instruction, they should focus on the important guiding questions for this phase. The teacher needs to identify the important mathematics that students must know in order to successfully complete the task. Teachers must then plan for developing a sense of what good mathematical communication looks like in written work. Teachers should also think about the tools they might emphasize to their students to help them organize and communicate information. For example, diagrams frequently illustrate important relationships and concepts. Students might be encouraged to incorporate diagrams into their writing, properly label the diagrams, and refer specifically to the diagram in their writing. These instructional tools will be discussed in more detail in later chapters.

Revising

Student Questions: Have I answered the question fully? Are my conjectures and ideas supported? Is my work clear and understandable?

Teacher Questions: Do students adequately justify and support their ideas? What instructional strategies will encourage and support clear and understandable writing?

Revising is an indispensable part of the writing process that should not be underemphasized in content area writing. Mathematics teachers understand the importance of verifying work—and of how difficult it is to get students to engage in this process. Research indicates that students routinely fail to verify the reasonableness or accuracy of their work (Lester, 1989; Pugalee, 2001a; Sexton & Ballew, 1988). Thus, emphasizing revision as an important part of writing and problem solving reinforces the mutual relationship between these thinking processes. It is hoped that revision and verification behaviors will become more commonplace as students realize that they are important parts of a larger process.

Always encourage students to make sure that they addressed the question being raised in the task or assignment. Sometimes students have well-written work that includes significant mathematical concepts and ideas, yet they may fail to specifically address the task. Such behaviors sometimes result in students losing points in formal writing assessments, such as those given by many state educational agencies. Students should reflect on their work to revisit how they used important mathematical concepts and ideas to support their work as well as the mathematical accuracy of those statements. As the teacher plans to make revision important, consideration should be given to planning instructional activities or strategies that address using mathematics to support and/or justify thinking. In addition, the teacher should provide opportunities for students to develop an understanding of clear and understandable writing. For example, a teacher might take a statement from a student's written work, making sure the student's identity remains undisclosed, and show how to make the statement(s) clearer and more understandable. The importance of modeling will be highlighted later in this chapter.

Figure 1-2 illustrates how the teachers' questions guide the planning of appropriate writing tasks in a lesson on angles and how to

Mathematical Target
Students will differentiate between types of angles.

Writing Task
Compare these angles:

Writing Phase	Teachers' Question(s)	Example
Planning	Are my writing assignments stated clearly and are the expectations communicated?	Add the following statement to clarify your expectations: Use appropriate terms and tell how you know each angle is a specific type of angle.
Composing	What is the important mathematical content that must be accessible to the student?	Students should know the difference between acute, obtuse, right, and straight angles. Students should recognize these types of angles without knowing angle measures or using a protractor.
	How can the written content reflect good mathematical thinking?	Students will use the terms *acute, obtuse, right,* and *straight.* Students will relate these terms to 90° and 180°.
	What strategies can I emphasis for organizing and communicating that information?	Emphasize labeling the diagrams, using important mathematical terms, and stating mathematical ideas and definitions in the answer.
Revising	Do students adequately justify and support their ideas?	Students' responses must include the correct label for the angle and an appropriate description. For example, for the first angle a student might argue that it is an obtuse angle because it folds out, making it more than 90°.
	What instructional strategies will encourage and support clear and understandable writing?	Model use of terms for angles and use 90° and 180° as references. Emphasize this language in various examples, such as rectangles, parallelograms, and triangles.

Figure 1-2.   Illustration of Teachers' Questions That Reinforce the Writing Process

consider relating those tasks to the three phases of the writing process. The teacher should emphasize the three phases and use the student questions to help students realize what their roles are in each of the phases. This explicit attention serves to reinforce not only the writing process but also good problem-solving behaviors.

Principle 2: Writing Has Different Purposes and Goals

Students should have opportunities to write for different purposes and goals: to inform, explain, describe, persuade, and entertain. Mathematics provides a context for students to appreciate the various goals for writing. This is an especially important idea to reinforce in mathematics, where the form of writing that has most frequently been emphasized is formal proof.

Although many writing experts refer to three goals for writing, this book will approach writing in mathematics from a standpoint of two broad purposes: transactive and literary.[4] One rationale for this position is the emphasis of transactive writing in the school curriculum. A second rationale is the underlying role of expressive writing in making students' learning personal. Expressive writing is writing for which the author is his or her own audience. Such informal writing is the foundation for putting thoughts onto paper and cuts across much of the writing that students will do when they conceptualize. This type of writing has an important role in promoting students' understanding of concepts and information. This form of writing is also underemphasized in the middle and secondary curriculum, although it is a major focus at the elementary level. Our emphasis will be on transactive and literary writing, but expressive writing will be emphasized throughout this book as a vehicle for making mathematics personal and relevant to the student.

Transactive writing includes texts that inform, explain, describe, and persuade. This form of writing is most indicative of the types of writing students will do in other courses, in college settings, and in realistic endeavors throughout their lives. The goal of such writing is to provide the reader with information that includes explanations, justifications, and supporting evidence. Such writing often includes examples, reasons, comparisons and contrasts, diagrams, charts, tables, facts, and illustrations that address the purpose of the writing and support any conclusions. Formats include letters, editorials, academic writing, newspaper articles, speeches, proposals, memos, and other forms of writing that are indicative of work. This will be the primary type of writing that students are likely to engage in while writing in mathematics.

Literary writing is writing to entertain. Such forms include songs, poems, stories, plays, and other creative endeavors. Personal writing deals with an individual's experiences. Such forms include autobiographical pieces, memoirs, and reflective writing. Autobiographical and memoir writing may focus on a single event or an idea and contain illustrations of life examples. Reflective writing draws the writer into considering his or her personal growth and development.

During the planning process, teachers should consider various types of writing assignments. Consider the learning targets or objectives for students, and develop writing exercises that address the important mathematical ideas in those competencies. Table 1-4 clarifies how learning targets (objectives) and the purpose for writing align.

Table 1-4.   Learning Target and Writing Purpose

Elementary Example
Learning Target: Students will compare benchmark fractions (halves, thirds, fourths) using models.
Writing Purpose: Descriptive—show understanding of these fractions and how they compare, using key terms such as *larger, smaller, more, less.*

Middle School Example
Learning Target: Students will identify and describe similar polygons.
Writing Purpose: Persuade or justify—demonstrate understanding of similarity by creating a justification for why two polygons are similar, using concepts involving proportionality of sides and equivalence of angle measures.

Secondary Example
Learning Target: Students will solve basic two-step equations.
Writing Purpose: Entertain—write a story that illustrates how equations can be solved by performing the same operation on both sides of the equal sign. (Unedited sample follows.)

I'm an Equals Sign…..

In Function Land I have an important job. You see - there has always been a rift between the left and right sides of this great state. My job is to guarantee that regardless of what happens, both sides are the same. This is difficult because my friends who deal in operations (like addition, subtraction, multiplication, and division – but there are others) are always changing the way things look. I have to make sure that when something gets changed on one side that another operation on the other side keeps things the same. Just the other day, two units were added to the right side of Function Land, I had to arrange for someone to add two units to the left side. I'm no longer an equals sign if I allow something done on one side to not balance the other. Can you imagine how it would be to lose your identity – not to mention your job…. The hardest part of my work is making sure the Variables keep things balanced. You see, I have to constantly check to make sure their value hasn't changed. I can do this by getting my friends in operations to do their jobs until I have nothing but variables on one side and numbers on the other…. Whew, sometimes that is a difficult task. So, you can see my job is important. Maybe the most import job in Function Land.

These examples show how learning targets and writing purposes align. The examples show how the purpose of writing is directly related to the mathematics that the teacher wants the student to understand. The elementary example illustrates the importance of writing tasks that incorporate the use of models. This is important because models play a significant role in illustrating important mathematical concepts and ideas. The middle school example shows how justification plays a pivotal role in helping students to apply important mathematical ideas and then demonstrate how they applied those ideas to arrive at mathematically sound conclusions. The secondary example helps to dispel the notion that writing to entertain has no educational value. A sample story is provided to demonstrate how writing to entertain can also satisfy the purpose of demonstrating students' understanding of important algebraic skills.

Principle 3: Writing Has Different Formats

Writing has different formats that are related to its purpose, goal, and audience. Students should have opportunities to produce writing in mathematics using these different formats. Why is the use of multiple formats important? Morgan (1998) presents arguments that students should be exposed to a wide variety of genres appropriate for mathematical writing. This reinforces the appropriate use of mathematical language and the expectations of the mathematics discipline. The argument is also made that explicit attention to language (such as through multiple writing forms) enables students, particularly those from less privileged backgrounds, to engage in mathematics on a more equal footing. Some formats and organizational characteristics that are likely to be found in various types of mathematical writing are described below. Although creative endeavors encourage other formats, the following descriptions provide a base for considering how various types of writing in mathematics might be organized. The goal is not to provide a template for writing assignments, but to raise awareness about possible formats.

Recounting

Narrative forms might best be viewed as stories about what one knows, what one doesn't know, and what one wishes to know (Meier & Rishel, 1998). These forms of writing infuse or summarize dialogue. The narrative forms give students an opportunity to write about their thoughts, tell a story, or describe events. The mathematical autobiography is one example of such writing; here students recount their experiences with mathematics. Other writing forms might appear more formal, such as using first-person narrative to retell how one approached a certain mathematical task or thought about a mathematical problem or situation. Narrative forms require the writer to observe, explore, and reflect on experiences. As such, narrative writing provides a foundation for helping the student to "own" and make sense of his or her mathematical experiences. As evidenced through the "I'm an Equals Sign" example in Table 1-4, narrative forms provide an outlet for students to demonstrate rather sophisticated mathematical notions. Narratives may be about either true or fictional events. Organization of content may be chronological or sequential, although other ways of arranging details are possible. Many forms of narrative writing contain an introduction, the presentation of a problem or an event, and a solution or an outcome. Other forms include diaries and journals, poems and songs, plays, and short stories.

Describing Procedures and Methods

We will consider this form of descriptive writing separate from narrative writing, although many writing experts often refer to descriptive writing as narrative in form. The type of descriptive writing that is the focus of this section requires the writer to describe by adding detail and information. It is a common form of mathematical writing in which the student describes the methods and procedures that were employed in solving a problem or considering a mathematical concept or idea. It is the form of writing that students often produce on assessments when they are asked to describe how they solved a problem. Students might write a description of how they solved a word problem, completed a certain computational problem, solved an equation, applied geometric or algebraic concepts and ideas, or completed some other type of mathematical task.

For example, a teacher can place various geometric figures in a bag so that the students cannot see them, then have the students write a description of the contents of the bag. This form of writing requires attention to detail and the use of powerful, concise, and appropriate mathematical vocabulary. It is frequently characterized by a step-by-step description of students' actions. Although this form of writing is most familiar to mathematics teachers and is an effective approach to support mathematical understanding, the other forms of writing must also receive consideration, for they also have tremendous potential to accomplish the goal of writing in mathematics, which is to help students become mathematically literate. When planning for writing in mathematics, teachers should make sure to use a range of writing formats.

Explaining

This form of mathematical writing requires students to give information, explain a mathematical concept or idea, or define or provide details about a term, law, postulate, or theorem. This form of writing draws on students' abilities to make reasonable conclusions using facts, data, examples, definitions, and mathematical principles and concepts to support the ideas. Explaining mathematical ideas to others requires careful thought about the conventional use of mathematical symbols, formulas, and notation and a deep understanding of the math that is being used. For example, in this form of mathematical writing, students might be asked to articulate the relationship between a table with data and a graph, or to explain how right-triangle relationships can be used in measuring distances. Students might describe how addition and multiplication are similar, or they might defend how their "line of best fit" is the best way to describe a set of data and predict other outcomes (a "line of best fit" is the line that best represents the trend of a data set). This writing is characterized by the presentation of a mathematical concept, conclusion, or idea that is followed by details and information that makes it clear.

Arguing

We're all probably familiar with this form of mathematical writing as the proofs of traditional high school geometry. This form of writing involves the use of cases or examples, the generalization of results, and sound mathematical reasoning that proves or explains how those generalizations are justified. Elementary students might be asked to argue, "Every other number can be broken into groups of twos." This is at a much different level of abstraction from asking a high school student to create an argument defending the statement "$2n$ is always even." Yet elementary students can create effective mathematical arguments even though they may depend on intuitive ideas and the use of pictures or diagrams. Such thinking is the hallmark of more formalized types of mathematical arguments.

The formats of writing involving explanation and argument may often have similar characteristics. The key characteristic is a reliance on mathematical justification to support ideas and actions. In writing an argument, students are supporting a generalization or conclusion by creating a mathematically sound justification for their ideas. Such writing might take the form of presenting cases and arguments that support stating a generalization or conclusion or stating a generalization or hypothesis and then creating an argument that supports the idea. One way of thinking of this format of writing is to consider how the traditional two-column proof from geometry might be presented in paragraph form.

Reporting

Formal mathematical reports provide opportunities to elaborate on mathematical concepts and demonstrate applications of mathematics, among other learning goals. Although mathematical reports may have different formats, the structure is similar to reports in other disciplines. Reports may contain an abstract summary of the contents of the paper, a problem statement, a body that develops several key ideas or concepts related to the problem, and a conclusion that succinctly summarizes the paper, including recommendations for additional research and implications such as applications. Reports end with a references section and possibly an appendix that contains information that is too lengthy to incorporate into the paper, such as raw data or lists. Reports may have different features, but the description presented here is a fairly standard format for such writing.

Principle 4:
Writing Has Different Audiences

Students begin writing in informal ways, and first-person accounts are predominant. Audiences for writing are generally progressive: writing for oneself, for the teacher, for a known audience (including peers), for an unknown audience, for a virtual known audience, and for an indiscernible audience. All of the various audiences for writing have a place in students' writing in mathematics; however, the majority of writing that students complete in mathematics will be for oneself, the teacher, or a known audience. The other audiences are not likely to be the focus.

Writing in which the audience is oneself is often problematic for the mathematics teacher because it is for personal benefit, and most writing assignments in mathematics are intended for the teacher's eyes. Nevertheless, there are times when writing strictly for oneself should be considered. For example, students might be asked to do a short "free-write" related to a mathematics lesson or topic, then follow through with one or more ideas selected from the writing. Students might also be asked to engage in writing that is solely for their own consumption, and teachers might devise ways to give credit for engaging in the process, but the writing remains the private discourse of the student. Teachers will have to decide how such writing fits within their instruction. More ideas will be considered in later chapters dealing with implementation and assessment. In sum, students should have some opportunities to engage in writing for which they will be the sole audience.

Writing for a wider audience requires a different set of considerations. The writer must determine what the audience might know and prepare his or her writing so that it clearly communicates the desired idea. Writing in which the teacher is the audience is probably most common. Students' writing is frequently produced with the understanding that the teacher will read what is produced. Such writing includes assessment pieces as well as formative pieces in which students engage in writing as a means of promoting the development of mathematical ideas, concepts, and skills. Writing with various goals and in various formats is appropriate for teachers to consider. When students write for the teacher, they must be aware of the teacher's expectations and how the teacher might assess their writing. In writing done for any audience, it is important that students develop some clear idea about what is necessary to meet the expectations for that particular audience.

Students are sometimes asked to write in mathematics for audiences other than oneself or the teacher. For the most part, these wider known audiences include peers, other professionals, parents, and other informal audiences. The same general rule applies: Students must write in a fashion that considers who the consumers of their product will be. Writing for peers is an important part in a mathematics program. Other instances in which the audience is known are assessment pieces at the local, state, or national level. Although the specific individuals are unknown, the student has enough information about the audience to respond in a way that anticipates the audience's expectations. Another audience for writing is parents and guardians; students might write particular pieces that they know will be reviewed by these individuals.

The other three audiences—unknown audience, virtual known audience, and indiscernible audience—are somewhat less likely for mathematics students. Although writing for an unknown audience is not likely, students might be given assignments in which they are encouraged to write for an audience that could potentially include anyone. Such writing requires a level of clarity and description that is inherently different from writing for more specific audiences. When the audience is not known, the writer must be careful to make sure that anyone could effectively read the information with success. Virtual known audiences include online audiences, such as those in e-mail groups or discussion-group posts. Such audiences are becoming an increasingly popular target for students writing about mathematics. Writing for an indiscernible audience is highly unlikely in mathematics. In general, there is some level of anticipation of who the readers will be. Writing in which the student has no information about the audience is highly unlikely.

Principle 5: Writing Should Be Done Often

This principle might be summed up using a commonly heard maxim: "Good writers are those who write often." This statement is no less true when we consider writing in mathematics. Students who have multiple opportunities to write about mathematics will be able to show marked growth in their level of mathematical understanding and their ability to communicate mathematically. When planning for instruction, teachers should consider frequent writing opportunities that provide students with the opportunities to become better at what mathematics writing is all about: presenting mathematical concepts, ideas, and procedures in ways that demonstrate a profound conceptual understanding—that is, mathematical literacy. The material presented here and in subsequent chapters provides details and strategies to help the mathematics teacher make writing a familiar component of mathematics instruction.

Modeling

Modeling is such an integral part of promoting writing in mathematics that it deserves some consideration as a basis for planning. Teachers need to consider how modeling fits into their instruction. Generally, modeling involves the teacher "walking through" an assignment or a task with the students. The teacher thinks aloud about what should be considered in producing the written product. Such brainstorming includes consideration of who the audience is and identification of key ideas that are essential to the task. The teacher might create a draft of the piece and model how to think about making revisions. Many elementary teachers often serve as scribes for students who do not have formal writing skills. Teachers at all levels can use scribing as a way of modeling the thinking process and how it is translated into a written product. The key questions presented for the writing stages earlier in this chapter can provide a framework for the teacher to model a writing task. The teacher is modeling the importance of the mathematical content and may decide to avoid an emphasis on mechanics. The teacher may even include some elements, concepts, or ideas that are inaccurate or flawed to model approaches for reflecting on, identifying, and fixing such elements.

Summary

In this chapter we have considered five principles that serve as a foundation for developing an effective program for writing in mathematics. These principles, some considerations about the phases of writing and their relationship to mathematics, and the importance of modeling writing in the mathematics' classroom provide a context for considering the goals of writing in mathematics. This context provides some key ideas and serves as a framework for instructional activities in mathematics with a writing focus. The ideas presented here are broad concerns that emphasize some basic questions that emerge when mathematics teachers begin to plan writing instruction. These ideas become a way of thinking about the relationship between writing and mathematics. How the teacher views that relationship will have an impact on how writing is designed, used, and assessed in the classroom. We hope that these considerations provide some basis for the instructional planning stage, in which the focus is not only identifying the important mathematics that students should know and understand but also developing conceptual understanding, thinking skills, and processes that help students to become truly mathematically literate.

Notes

1. Writing is one of many strategies that the teacher can utilize to impact the effectiveness of mathematics instruction. Other tools are also important. The process of providing instruction is complex. A rigorous mathematics program engages students in developing both conceptual and procedural knowledge. The National Council of Teachers of Mathematics is the professional organization for mathematics teachers. Three NCTM documents provide some key ideas about mathematics teaching and learning: *Professional Standards for Teaching Mathematics* (1991), *Assessment Standards for School Mathematics* (1995), and *Principles and Standards for School Mathematics* (2000).

2. The ideas presented here are not intended to oversimplify the complex process of language development nor the multifaceted relationship between language and mathematics. Those who want to further explore perspectives on language and mathematics should consult Steinbring, Bussi, and Sierpinska (1998) and Cobb, Yackel, and McClain (2000).

3. Authentic tasks may be conceptualized along four dimensions: thinking and reasoning, discourse, mathematical tools, and attitudes and dispositions (Pugalee, Douville, Lock, & Wallace, 2002). These types of tasks engage students in exploring mathematics through situational problems, grounded in real-life problems:

   - *Thinking and reasoning*—engaging in such activities as gathering data, exploring, investigating, interpreting, reasoning, modeling, designing, analyzing, formulating hypotheses, using trial and error, generalizing, and verifying outcomes.
   - *Discourse*—engaging in individual, small-group, and whole-class interactions; role of language and interactions in the construction of mathematical meaning.
   - *Mathematical tools*—using symbol systems such as tables, graphs, and drawings, and technological tools such as calculators, computers, and manipulatives.
   - *Attitudes and dispositions*—developing self-regulation, persistence, reflection, and enthusiasm (Pandey, 1990).

4. The purposes of writing sometimes appear with different terms. For example, some use the terms *expository, persuasive,* and *narrative.* Others use *informative* or *descriptive* when referring to expository writing. *Expressive* writing involves telling a story and often lacks the technical aspects of writing found in other purposes. Expressive writing has a place in mathematics classrooms. It is not the intent here to deemphasize this form of writing. Although expressive writing is important, and arguably the foundation for the development of writing and thinking in general, writing in mathematics will primarily consist of other forms of writing; therefore, transactive and literary forms will be emphasized.

Constructing Effective Exercises and Activities

This chapter begins with descriptions about the level of complexity in students' mathematical communication as they progress through school. This description underscores how vital the development of mathematical communication at one grade level is to students' successful communication at more advanced levels. Developing and modifying tasks that promote rich mathematical communication is the focus of this chapter. Considering text features, questioning, and developing writing prompts provides a focus on skills and strategies for constructing writing tasks. These guidelines and strategies will assist in constructing writing exercises and activities that support learning targets and help students in their development of mathematical literacy.

Developing Communication Across Grade Levels

In the early elementary grades, students have greater facility in speaking and listening than they do in writing (NCTM, 2000). Communication at these early levels involves an informal use of mathematical language in everyday conversations and in classroom talk. Students who are encouraged to explain their thinking as well as to listen to and think about peers' and teachers' thinking have unique opportunities to develop skills that provide a solid foundation for more formalized communication tasks, including speaking and writing. Students at these early grade levels can also be encouraged to use appropriate vocabulary as they share mathematical understanding in the classroom, as well as to begin to associate their drawings and illustrations with mathematical ideas and thoughts. These associations become important as students begin to engage in mathematical writing and other forms of communication that often meaningfully incorporate illustrations, drawings, constructions, diagrams, graphs, tables, and other graphics.

Students in grades 3 through 5 are developing flexibility in language use, especially the ability to use written communication. These students can write about mathematical solutions, conjectures, questions, and ideas. Students move beyond a natural and customary use of talk to discuss ideas, particularly as they solve mathematics problems with their peers. Students should begin to develop skills in expressing those ideas and thoughts in written form. Teachers at these grade levels focus more on students' effective and ineffective communication practices. Modeling of excellent written mathematics communication is especially important during these years, as students' writing skills become more refined and expectations are internalized. Mathematical vocabulary and expressions should become more evident, and teachers should take advantage of opportunities to introduce and reinforce proper use of mathematical language, including mathematical symbols. Expectations for correct, complete, coherent, and clear writing should be emphasized, including providing students with opportunities to revise their writing. Discussing and sharing students' approaches are effective means of developing flexibility and capacity for written language.

During middle school, grades 6 through 8, written communication is an essential means for students to express their mathematical thinking. The mathematics is becoming more abstract, and students' abilities to evaluate others' responses are also more refined. Adolescents in particular need a safe learning environment where they perceive that their ideas can be shared and challenged without it being personal. Written communication should include numerous opportunities to "think through problems, formulate explanations, try out new vocabulary or notation, experiment with forms of argumentation, justify conjectures, critique justifications, and reflect on their own understanding and on the ideas of others" (NCTM, 2000, p. 272). Students should also become engaged more frequently in writing tasks that require pairs or groups of students to formulate ideas and construct a common written response.

As students move to high school, they will have greater challenges in sharing and exchanging ideas and information. Students are also expected to demonstrate reasoning and communication skills that are appropriate for constructing effective mathematical arguments and formal as well as informal proofs. The need for thinking and writing that demonstrates logical chains of reasoning are more prevalent. Accurate use of mathematical vocabulary and notation are expected. Students at this level should have tremendous flexibility in speaking, hearing, reading, and writing mathematical ideas. See NCTM (2000) for a rich discussion of communication at the various grade levels.

Rich Communication Tasks

The goal of writing in mathematics is to engage students in ways that require them to think deeply about the mathematics they are encountering. You might think of writing tasks and the level of engagement as movement along some type of continuum from simple, mechanical responses to extended responses that require higher order thinking (Figure 2-1). At all grade levels, mathematical communication that is characteristic of various locations along this continuum can be emphasized. At the earliest grades, it is expected that some of the emphasis will be on oral communication as a means of demonstrating and developing mathematical understanding. As students develop writing skills, they can better take advantage of writing as a tool for developing mathematical understanding. However, the continuum is not about writing ability but about the level of cognitive engagement of the student. At one end of this continuum are rich writing tasks that provide students with opportunities to extend their thinking and make connections between and among mathematical concepts, ideas, and processes. At the other end of this continuum are writing tasks that reinforce isolated and disconnected development of mathematical understanding. The types of writing tasks given to students are important. The types of writing tasks become a significant factor in how effective those experiences are in promoting students' development of mathematical literacy.

One-word or short responses	Extended responses
Focus on facts, definitions, and procedures	Focus on evaluating, analyzing, justifying, and other higher order processes

Figure 2-1. Continuum of Engagement

Mathematics textbooks have begun to provide elements that focus on communication, including written forms. Most texts, however, provide few questions and exercises that call for communicating more than a final answer. A review of two introductory algebra texts from major publishers found few questions requiring students to communicate their mathematical thinking (Pugalee, Bissell, Lock, & Douville, 2003). Exercises and problems that required students to communicate often requested only short or one-word answers, factual phrases, simple descriptions, and definitions. Although the use of short answers and the reinforcement of definitions and facts are important, such types of exercises do not often encourage students to make associations among important mathematical concepts, procedures, and problems. Exercises that require students to write extended responses are more likely to encourage students to think deeply about the underlying mathematics.

Consider the following examples. Think about the level of mathematical thinking that these types of exercises promote.

> Fill in the blanks and give a reason for each step to complete a convincing argument that the power of a power property is true.
>
> $(a^2)^3 = a^2 \times ? \times ?$
>
> $\quad = ? \times ? \times ? \times ? \times ? \times ?$
>
> $\quad = ?$

This problem requires students to think deeply about the mathematics that they are applying. This is a much richer experience than just providing the answers that fill in the blanks. Students are asked to give a reason that supports their actions. Explaining the process behind the procedures helps students to remember why they are doing particular actions and helps them to develop a conceptual understanding of the mathematics being taught. In this problem, students must explain why

$$(a^2)^3 = a^2 \times a^2 \times a^2$$
$$\quad = a \times a \times a \times a \times a \times a$$
$$\quad = a^6$$

Their reasoning will engage them in explaining the role of powers. Through writing students will develop an understanding of the processes involved in this important mathematical procedure. Giving a reason for each step will require students to understand that a^2 raised to the third power means that it should be used as a factor three times. Then a^2 means a multiplied by a so that breaking this down for each a^2 produces a used as a factor six times. A short way of writing this is a^6. It is clear that the level of reasoning required to explain the power raised to a power property is much more engaging and provides the teacher with clearer indicators of what students really know about the procedures they use in class.

When considering the types of mathematical writing tasks to use, teachers should think about how the activities promote students' development of mathematical literacy, a deep level of mathematical understanding. The following components serve as some thinking points on the appropriateness of writing tasks to promote the type of mathematical learning that results in a conceptual understanding of mathematical concepts and processes. These five components (Kilpatrick, Swafford, & Findell, 2001) include the following:

- *Conceptual understanding:* focus on concepts, operations and relations.

- *Procedural fluency:* focus on completing procedures, but emphasis on developing flexibility, accuracy, efficiency, and appropriateness.

- *Strategic competence:* focus on formulating, representing, and solving problems.

- *Adaptive reasoning:* focus on developing logical thought processes, reflective thinking, and facility with explanations, descriptions, and justifications.

- *Productive dispositions:* focus on mathematics as sensible, useful, and worthwhile, and associated with students' positive views about their ability to engage in doing mathematics.

What happens when text materials provide little or no support for writing in mathematics? This chapter will discuss some of those issues and offer some strategies. The point thus far is that texts offer such exercises at various levels, and teachers should take advantage of those opportunities by recognizing how such exercises can engage students and require thinking that goes beyond rote work involving computations and procedures. The discussion on rich tasks provides key points not only in considering the nature of tasks found in textbooks and other resources but also in the teacher's construction of writing tasks to support learning goals.

Using Text Features to Support Written Communication

Most mathematics texts have some common features. Understanding these features and their purpose can help in thinking about ways to make those features support writing in mathematics. First, there is not much text to read, but the small amount of text carries conceptually dense information, frequently in no more than five to seven sentences. Sections may contain diagrams, cases, models, or illustrations that are used to clarify or broaden the information being presented. These figures emphasize the ideas presented in the short text passages and are fundamental to developing a solid understanding of the concept(s) being discussed. These features may be interspersed with definitions, rules, and formulas. Before students are presented with problems and exercises, they are generally given several examples applying the mathematical concepts and ideas. These text features differ dramatically from those in other subject areas, often creating difficulty for students to process at a level that demonstrates basic comprehension. Writing provides a tool to assist students in using text features to understand the mathematics being presented. Table 2-1 illustrates how this can be done.

Table 2-1.   Modifying Text Features to Support Writing

Text Feature	Modification for Promoting Writing
Conceptually Dense Information	Restating and/or summarizing important concepts or ideas.
Diagrams, Cases, Models, & Illustrations	Descriptive writing that requires students to incorporate diagrams and illustrations into a problem or explain how a diagram or illustration supports the mathematical concept or idea being emphasized.
Definitions, Rules, & Formulas	Stating definitions, rules, or formulas in one's own words. Explaining why a rule or formula works.
Examples, Problems, & Procedures	Describing how examples are similar and different. Describing how examples demonstrate definitions, rules, formulas, etc.
Problems & Exercises	Extending exercises by asking students to tell *why* and *how* to explain and give reasons for their actions. What mathematics supports their actions? Telling what they did at each step and why.

A common lesson in elementary texts involves adding fractions with unlike denominators. A popular text approaches the lesson in the following way. First, the student is presented with a situation in which adding two fractions is necessary. Based on a class survey, the most popular flavors of ice cream were chocolate ($\frac{1}{3}$ of students) and vanilla ($\frac{1}{6}$ of students). Students are asked what part of the class preferred these two flavors.[1] Next, the necessary steps are presented for finding the answer: (a) Write fractions with the same denominators, (b) add the numerators, and (c) simplify the answer. The text now presents the process for answering what part of the class prefers chocolate and vanilla ice cream. This is followed by additional worked examples, with one problem written vertically and one written horizontally. Both examples involve fractions with unlike denominators. Each problem is then rewritten with common denominators and the final answer given. The process is not elaborated upon further; finding equivalent fractions was the topic of a previous lesson. The last two sections feature 10 problems for classwork followed by 30 problems in a practice section, with two problems presented as word problems.

Consider how writing can provide a tool for meaningfully engaging students in this lesson. For each part of the lesson, several ideas are presented. These examples show how writing can enhance students' conceptual development related to adding fractions. Teachers may select one or two writing tasks related to the lesson. Table 2-2 shows the types of questions constructed, which will relate to ideas that will be presented later.

In the first example, the questions help to orient the student to the problem. Understanding fractions is difficult for many students. The questions constructed to go with the opening scenario are designed to reinforce key ideas that students should develop about fractions. Students should understand that fractions are part-whole relationships. The questions reinforce these ideas. The second question extends that understanding by asking students to create a visual model for the two fractions. Students, particularly at the elementary level, need opportunities to visualize abstract information. It is a good practice to ask students to incorporate visual models and diagrams into their work. Such practices help students to move beyond procedural understanding toward conceptually understanding the process involved in adding two fractions (Cramer, Post & del Mas, 2002).[2] This model can be used later during the lesson, to reinforce ideas about common denominators and to help students see how the two fractions combine to give $\frac{1}{2}$.

Table 2-2.   Writing to Support Text Features

Text Information	Writing Prompts to Extend Text
Students presented with scenario: 1/3 of students prefer chocolate ice cream and 1/6 prefer vanilla ice cream. What part of the class prefers chocolate and vanilla ice cream?	• What does the fraction 1/3 mean? • Use circles or squares to show 1/3 and 1/6. How can you tell which is larger?
Worked example using ice cream scenario	• What does the fraction 3/6 mean? How would this relate to a class of 24 students? • Show how 3/6 and 1/2 represent the same fraction. Write a few sentences explaining your work.
Additional worked examples	• Write the steps for this problem. • Why do you not add the denominators when adding fractions?
Classwork problems	• The first problem is 2/5 + 1/5. If someone gets 1/5 as the answer, what did they probably do wrong? • Describe how you find a common denominator for 1/4 and 1/3.
Practice problems	• Tell how you worked problem 3 (a selected problem from the text). • Draw a diagram and tell how you know your answer for number 3 (a selected problem from the text) is correct.

The next suggestions extend students' thinking about the task. Notice that the first prompt consists of two questions. The second question extends the idea inherent in the first one; otherwise, students may simply describe the idea of the part-whole relationship without thinking about the context. Students need to understand how $3/6$ relates to the problem. The question will engage them in thinking about the part-whole relationship and developing their proportional understanding. If 3 out of 6 students prefer chocolate or vanilla ice cream, that would be 12 students in a group of 24. The second example asks students to show how $1/2$ and $3/6$ represent the same fraction. This prompt helps students to understand the mathematics being used and assists them in justifying their thinking. Students' work with models once again supports building conceptual understanding of important concepts, particularly the notion of equivalence of fractions.

The next ideas emphasize the purpose of worked examples in mathematics texts. The goal is to make sure that students understand the procedures and concepts presented in the lesson. The possible prompts emphasize these goals by having students write the steps used in the example. This will help to reinforce those steps with an example that is already worked, allowing students to internalize the steps necessary to be successful with the problems. Procedures are important, but students must also develop a conceptual understanding of what they are doing. Writing provides a tool to accomplish both those goals. Notice in the second suggestion that students are asked to tell why the denominators are not added when adding two fractions. The goal is to focus on the procedures being emphasized in the worked examples and to extend the conceptual ideas behind those procedures.

The examples for classwork and practice problems have a similar focus, to help students reflect on the procedures being used and verify their solutions. By asking students to write about their thinking, they are required to reflect on what they are doing and how those actions make sense mathematically. Notice that one of the prompts focuses on a common error that students may commit—subtracting instead of adding the fractions. Teachers can substitute other common errors, such as adding the denominators together when adding two fractions. The goal is to make students aware of common errors and to focus their thinking on the tasks. If students can verify their solution to a practice problem, they will have greater confidence to proceed with other problems. Some teachers find that when they begin giving students this type of writing task, many students feel more comfortable if they are given the answer to the problem. As students become more confident in describing their thinking and justifying their work, teachers may provide less support. The goal is to promote thinking about the process of adding fractions.

Questioning That Engages Students

Questioning is an important part of a teacher's repertoire of strategies that can be used effectively to engage students, focus them on important mathematical concepts and principles, and challenge them to extend their thinking. NCTM (1991) advocates mathematics classrooms that empower students. One element of this empowerment is the use of questions to help students understand and appreciate mathematics and thus develop mathematical literacy. Although questioning is characteristically part of the oral exchange that occurs in the classroom, think of the categories and examples in Table 2-3 (see NCTM, 1991) as possibilities not only for stimulating students' thinking through verbal questions but also to engage students in written communication.

Table 2-3. Questions for Building Mathematical Understanding

Students Working Together to Make Sense of Mathematics
- What does the class think about what a particular student said?
- Do you agree? Disagree? Why?
- Do you understand what he or she is saying? Could you summarize his or her ideas?
- Does anyone have the same answer but a different way to explain it?
- Can you convince the rest of us that what you are saying makes sense mathematically?

Students Relying on Themselves to Justify Their Thinking
- Why do you think that?
- Why is that true?
- How did you reach that conclusion?
- Does that make sense? Why?
- Can you make a model to illustrate that?

Students Learning to Reason Mathematically
- Does that always work?
- Is that true in other cases? All cases?
- Can you think of an example that wouldn't work (a counterexample)?
- How could you create an argument to support that?
- What assumptions are you making?

Students Learning to Conjecture, Invent, and Problem-Solve
- What would happen if . . . ?
- Can you describe a pattern?
- What are some possibilities?
- Tell how you can predict the next one.
- How did you think about the problem?
- What decision do you think one should make?
- What is the same or different about your method and the other student's?

Students Connecting Mathematics With Its Ideas and Applications
- How does this relate to . . . ?
- What ideas that we studied before were helpful in this problem or situation?
- Have we solved a problem similar to this before?
- What are some ways this mathematics might be applied in the real world?
- Can you provide an example of . . . ?

The types of questions provided in the table provide a rich entry point for mathematical communication. Notice the centrality of mathematical reasoning in these questions. The types of questions that focus mathematics instruction and promote higher order thinking are also good foundations for creating prompts and exercises for writing in mathematics. Excellent writing prompts do not have to be disjointed from the important mathematical understanding that is the focus of instruction. Students can be asked to write responses to these questions. If students are frequently asked to respond to such questions in their day-to-day classroom discussions, their facility with written communication will be much better. Questions such as these, which promote mathematical understanding, provide an effective means for teachers to make written communication an integral part of how mathematics is developed, supported, and extended in the classroom.

The following examples show how questioning can transform a task with a single answer into an opportunity for students to reason mathematically. Three examples are presented along with a discussion. One example is presented from each of the grade bands: K–2, 3–5, and 6–8. The examples clarify how writing extends students' thinking about mathematics by involving them in higher order thinking that promotes mathematical literacy.

How Many Children Are on the Playground? (K–2)

In response to the problem "There are 5 boys and 4 girls on the playground. Mr. Love brings his class of 23 students outside. Now how many children are on the playground?" a second grader answered with Figure 2-2.

Students in early elementary grades do not have the capacity to write long responses to mathematics problems. Yet this is an important time for students to begin developing important mathematical communication skills. Many early elementary students will incorporate diagrams or pictures into their responses. These representations provide important clues about how the students are thinking about the problem. Notice that this second grader's response to the playground problem uses diagrams. First, she draws some lines to illustrate the playground—not necessarily an important piece of information, as far as solving the mathematics problem, but an important contextual feature that shows the student understands the situation in which the problem took place. Then the student selects

I saw children and I counted one at a time thats how I got the Answer.

playGround

boys
OOOOO
Girls
l l l l

mr.Love's
m m m m m m m Cla:
m m m m m
m m m m m
m m m m m
m m

Figure 2-2. Second-Grade Response

a different way of representing the various quantities: circles for the five boys, sticks for the four girls, and *M*s for the 23 students in Mr. Love's class. This use of different symbols to show the quantities tells us something about the student's understanding of groupings. There are three distinct quantities in the problem, with each representing a different group of students, and this doesn't get lost in how the student chose to tell about her solution. This helped her so that she "saw children" and then "counted one at a time." Writing provided the student an opportunity to show how she thought about additive situations that involved quantities from three groups. The visual elements the student selects to represent her thinking show how powerful visual images are for students, especially students who are developing important number-concept understanding.

The Equilateral Triangle Garden (3–5)

For the problem "A garden is shaped like an equilateral triangle. It took 54 feet of fence to enclose the garden. What is the length of one side of the garden?" a fifth grader responded with Figure 2-3.

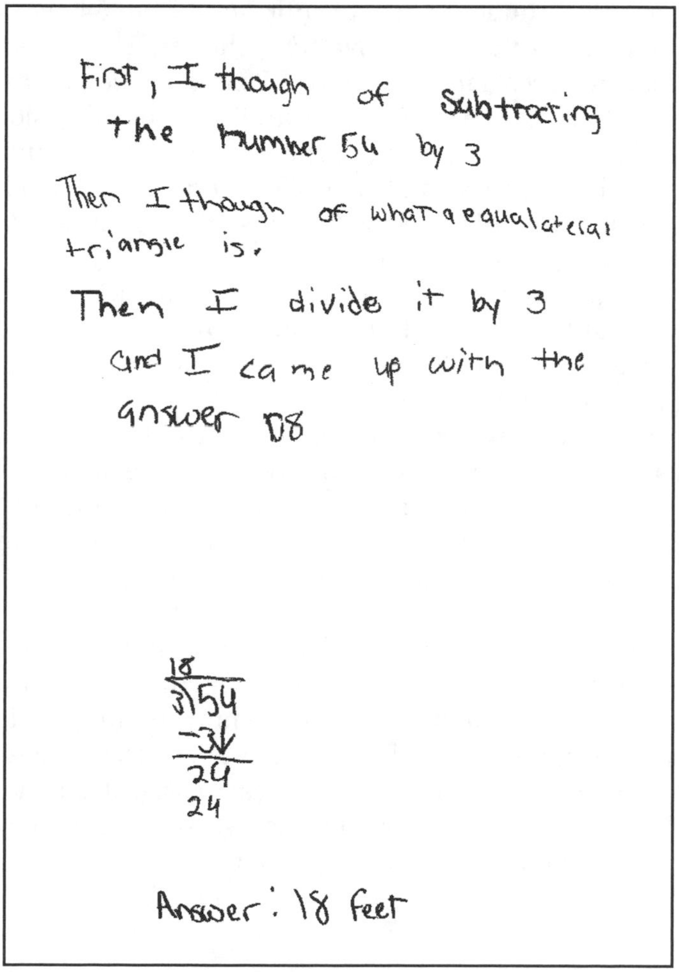

First, I though of subtracting the number 54 by 3

Then I though of what a equalateral triangle is.

Then I divide it by 3 and I came up with the answer 18

$$\begin{array}{r} 18 \\ 3\overline{)54} \\ -3\downarrow \\ \hline 24 \\ 24 \end{array}$$

Answer: 18 feet

Figure 2-3. Fifth-Grade Response

Problems of this nature provide great opportunities to get a glimpse of the thinking of students. Just getting a numerical answer from the student tells little about how the student thought about the problem. In this example, the fifth-grade teacher had asked the students to describe what went on "inside your head" when they solved the problem. It was given rather early in the year, and at this point the students had limited experience with writing in mathematics; nevertheless, this student provides some interesting insights. First, he thought about "subtracting the number 54 by 3." The student abandons this line of reasoning, but his initial comment is interesting. Student ideas of this nature are the types of comments that provide starting points for interesting discussions.

Notice that the student didn't say to subtract 3 from 54, but to subtract 54 by 3. The teacher followed up with this student later and realized that the student meant to subtract 3 from 54 over and over. When asked what that would give him, the student replied that he knew he had to "break it into threes." There are some parallels between the operations of subtraction and division. Division may be viewed as repeated subtraction, in the same way that multiplication may be viewed as repeated addition. This student's initial idea wasn't so far off base after all. The student just didn't know where to go with the results of his initial idea.

Note too that the student doesn't provide all this information in his writing, but the teacher follows up because she is curious about what the student meant. The student does, however, reconsider the meaning of an equilateral triangle.

In later chapters, we will discuss what the teacher might do to extend students' writing. A more comprehensive response would have included some indication of the meaning of an equilateral triangle. Many students responding to this prompt did include a diagram that demonstrated an understanding that the three sides of the triangle were equal.

The student finally decides to divide by 3 and arrives at an answer of 18 feet. Notice that the student includes the unit of measure—an important component in measurement problems. The written description provides information about the process the student used. It also shows how writing can assist students in being more reflective. With this response, the student is forced to reconsider his ideas and abandon an approach.

The Triangular Number Problem (Middle School)

Figurate number problems can be found in most middle-grade mathematics books. Figurate numbers are formed by placing dots in a geometric figure, such as a triangle, a square, a rectangle, or a pentagon. The student in Figure 2-4 is from a seventh-grade mathematics class. She is asked to tell which number comes next—requiring a single answer. The problem was modified by a classroom teacher who asked the students to tell how they arrived at the answer.

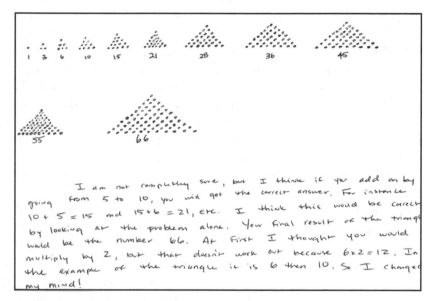

Figure 2-4.   Seventh-Grade Response

Pam's response indicates how transforming this one-answer exercise provided an opportunity to see how she was thinking about the problem. In her response, we can see that she struggled with alternative answers but realized that they did not meet the conditions in the problem. She realizes that each number is the previous total plus a new line of dots that increases by 1 for each number. "Add on by going from 5 to 10, you will get the correct answer. For instance, 10 + 5 = 15 and 15 + 6 = 21, etc."

Having students reflect on the nature of the patterns and then describe them is important in developing students' algebraic thinking. Students' work with patterns should include opportunities to describe patterns in general terms and justify those generalizations as a foundation for pre-algebra and algebra and as one way of fostering algebraic thinking (Driscoll, 1999).[3] A single-answer response would have limited students' thinking about the problem, and they would have missed a learning opportunity to extend and develop their mathematics reasoning skills.

The Beginning, Middle, and End of Class Considerations

Typical lessons follow general patterns, with characteristic activities at the beginning, middle, and end of the lesson. Considering these patterns as ways of thinking about writing in the mathematics classroom may prove fruitful. Regardless of the type of thinking you employ when you consider the elements of a mathematics lesson, there are some general goals for various parts of a lesson. These may be repeated as often as necessary, particularly in block scheduling situations; nevertheless, these time frames are generally marked by characteristic teaching and learning goals. Although the patterns are general, some lessons may require very different trajectories. This section will provide some ideas for short writing tasks that take only a few minutes but support important learning objectives.

The beginning of a mathematics lesson most frequently contains some development of the focus of the lesson and an appropriate review of the concepts and ideas. Students should develop some idea of what they are expected to understand by the end of the lesson, and they frequently need some review of previous concepts and lessons. Activating prior knowledge helps students to apply what they have learned to new contexts.

Following are some ideas for writing in mathematics during the first part of the lesson. These are short writing tasks and can be used to get students on task as quickly as possible.

- Use a prompt such as "Write what you know about ____" to see what students might already know about related concepts and ideas. (A lesson on parallelograms might ask students to write what they know about parallel lines.) These can be used to introduce the concepts in the lesson.

- Have students write a short description of how they solved a particular homework problem. This is a good way to focus students immediately on thinking about previous mathematics work. As part of the review, have one or two students share their work.

- Present students with new terms to be encountered in the day's lesson. Students might copy these and begin to think about their meanings. It might be too early to ask students to restate them in their own words, but you can pair this activity with one at the end of class in which they revisit the formal definitions and rewrite them in their own words.

- Students can identify in two or three sentences the particular problems they encountered in the previous lesson. These can be collected, copied and distributed, and discussed as part of the review.

The largest segment of mathematics lessons focuses on concept development. The goal here is to help students make sense of the mathematics they are encountering in the day's lesson. The following ideas show how writing can support the teacher in helping each student to develop a conceptual understanding of the mathematics.

- Have students write an example or draw a diagram or other illustration to demonstrate a key idea or concept. For example, elementary students studying counting by twos might be asked to make a drawing or diagram to show how they would count a dozen items.

- Have students write a question about a concept or problem, then turn to another classmate and exchange questions. Students can respond and discuss their approaches. This helps to identify confusion and supports students in understanding the lesson. Teachers can circulate and follow up in whole-class discussion if common problems or misunderstandings emerge.

- If students are taking notes, pause and have them write a summary of an idea or concept in the margin. One or more good examples could be shared with the class.

The last part of a mathematics lesson provides opportunities for students to reflect on their learning and apply the concepts and ideas. Short writing tasks can be used to provide a mechanism for students to think about key ideas and concepts.

- Write the main idea from the day's lesson. Students can share these as a way of wrapping up the lesson.

- Write definitions in your own words. This might also apply to a procedure or property. Teachers may want to use caution to make sure the students have the important ideas. It might be useful to talk about key words or ideas that should be part of the writing.

- Have students exchange notes, a practice problem, or another task. Students can identify common elements and approaches as well as differences. Use class discussion or reporting to make sure that students have captured essential concepts and ideas. Encourage students to improve their notes, problems, or tasks. If writing wasn't part of the task, have students identify something they changed during the lesson and tell why. If they didn't change anything, they can write one or two sentences telling why they are mathematically confident of their work.

Prompts to Guide Mathematical Writing

One way of extending the discussion about the types of prompts that guide students' writing in mathematics is to think of the primary learning goal of the task. (Learning mathematics is always a goal, but there may be others as well). Writing applications in mathematics primarily include one of five goals: developing students' knowledge of mathematics, developing problem-solving methods, developing self-monitoring and reflective behaviors, promoting affective issues, and promoting discourse. Table 2-4 provides some possible prompts to guide the construction of writing tasks specific to these goals (Pugalee, 1998).

Table 2-4.   Writing Prompts Aligned to Learning Targets

Developing Students' Knowledge of Mathematics
- Write personal definitions of terms, rules, and theorems.
- Write explanations of mathematical concepts and ideas.
- Write a summary of a lesson or task.
- Write explanations of errors. (What went wrong? How can the error be addressed?)
- Offer examples and justify selection.
- Describe rules, their application, and mathematical importance.

Developing Problem-Solving Methods
- Write problems, applications, and provide solutions.
- Describe how to solve a problem.
- Compare and contrast alternative approaches to a problem.
- Describe how technology helped in finding a solution. (Describe the mathematical processes required for the output.)
- Write a formal report for approaching a problem situation.

(Continued)

Table 2-4.   Writing Prompts Aligned to Learning Targets *(Continued)*

Developing Self-Monitoring and Reflective Behaviors

- Describe what made a problem or task easy and/or difficult.
- Explain why an answer or a solution is reasonable.
- Identify and react to questions one may raise about your work (or respond to a question someone raised about your work).
- Analyze the quality of one's work (process, methods, mathematical soundness, communication).
- Describe how different decisions might impact an answer.
- Describe how problems are similar and/or different.

Promoting Affective Issues

- Write an autobiography about a mathematics experience.
- Write about the role mathematics plays in your life or might play in the future.
- Describe how mathematics changes or changed your life.
- Explain what helps or hinders you in understanding mathematics.
- Describe how you feel about your performance on a task or problem.

Promoting Discourse

- Write a note to the teacher for additional information.
- Specify lesson components that were not understood or components that you understood well.
- Write a journal entry about some aspect of the day's class.
- Summarize a topic, problem, or other mathematically related idea with a peer.
- Write a response to a problem or task for a group.

Fifty additional suggestions appear in Table 2-5. The suggestions are meant to be a starting point for adding to and revising a growing repertoire of strategies based on personal classroom experiences and curricular demands.

Table 2-5.   50 Activities for Writing in Mathematics

1. Summarize part of a class discussion or lecture.
2. Summarize part of the text.
3. Keep learning logs of key concepts.
4. Use key words in an explanation or a description.
5. Construct test or quiz questions.
6. Write freely on any topic.
7. Defend a decision or action.
8. Create a dialogue between one student and another.
9. Describe a graph or table.
10. List characteristics or steps.
11. Compare your understanding of a concept to what you knew before a lesson or exercise.

(Continued)

Table 2-5. 50 Activities for Writing in Mathematics *(Continued)*

12. Write a proposal for a project.
13. Write a children's story using a math concept.
14. Summarize an interview related to a math topic.
15. Write a biographical sketch of a mathematician.
16. Paraphrase a section of text.
17. Write a memo dealing with a math topic or problem.
18. Create and defend projections of what might happen in a number of days, months, or years.
19. Identify personal goals for mathematics learning.
20. Create examples of a concept.
21. Write critiques of a process or an approach.
22. Use mapping or another graphic organizer to identify key ideas and associations.
23. Write a response to a question, comment, or quotation.
24. Use double-entry notes—notes on one side, reflections on the other.
25. Create a simile or metaphor (e.g., Equations are like scales).
26. Keep a journal.
27. Write a commercial or an ad using mathematics.
28. Write a mathematics word problem.
29. Write a letter explaining a mathematical idea, problem, or process.
30. Write an autobiography related to mathematics or when one might have applied a particular concept (e.g., what mathematics have you used in sports, travel, or a hobby).
31. Develop an argument supporting an approach.
32. Find and describe a contradiction.
33. Prepare an outline of a lesson.
34. Find an example of mathematics in a novel, a newspaper, or another reading. Summarize the problem and describe the mathematics being used.
35. Describe how two problems are similar and/or different.
36. Write the definition of a term given in class or the text. Rewrite it in your own words. Tell how your own definition includes all the important information.
37. Analyze another student's work. Tell whether you agree or disagree with his or her conclusion and why.
38. Select a homework problem that gave you some difficulty. Write about what gave you difficulty and how you understand the idea, concept, or process now.
39. Write a poem or song about a math topic.
40. List what you know about a math topic (e.g., odd numbers, exponents, addition of fractions, equations).
41. Write several questions that are important to ask yourself when doing a particular type of problem (e.g., dividing two fractions, solving a word problem, graphing a quadratic equation).
42. Create a drawing or an illustration to a problem. Describe how they are related.
43. Explain how to use a calculator or other tool to help solve a problem.
44. Compile a list of unfamiliar terms in a lesson. Follow up with definitions and examples.
45. Use Venn diagrams or concept cards.
46. Describe how a concrete example or manipulative helped in understanding a concept.
47. Write a summary of major points on using notes to study for a quiz or test.
48. Write an editorial or a letter to the editor using mathematics to make a point.
49. Compose an e-mail describing a mathematics concept or idea.
50. Write a description of how you located an error in a problem, or a misconception in an idea, and how you corrected it.

Summary

The level of complexity in students' mathematical communication increases across the grade levels. Students move from an informal use of language, which might be characterized by pictures and other diagrams, to a more formalized writing, which demonstrates a clear line of argument and logic. Teachers should consider the writing abilities of their students when constructing tasks for mathematics, and the tasks should be appropriate. Teachers of younger students may develop tasks that build on responses of a few words and that incorporate pictures or other visuals. As students' writing skills become more refined, teachers can expect students' written products in mathematics to mirror their growing written communication skills.

Textbooks often fail to provide tasks that emphasize communication. Although textbook publishers are doing a much better job, many mathematics texts do not provide adequate support for developing mathematical communication. The nature of mathematics texts is to present conceptually dense concepts and ideas in a few sentences that are often interspersed with diagrams, illustrations, and examples. This is often followed by worked problems or applications of concepts or procedures before students are given problems of their own to tackle. The strategies and ideas presented in this chapter, along with a discussion of writing in the beginning, middle, and end of mathematics lessons, will help in designing writing tasks that support instructional goals. The key idea is that writing tasks should support instruction and help students to understand the mathematics being developed. When writing tasks engage students and focus on developing a conceptual understanding of mathematics, students will become mathematically literate.

Notes

1. This is a typical setup found in mathematics textbooks. Most texts arrange lessons using these same features. The scenario has been modified for demonstration.

2. In this study, a project was implemented emphasizing the use of physical models and translations between various modes of representation (pictorial, manipulative, verbal, real-world, and symbolic). Students who used this program had higher mean scores on a posttest and retention test of four subscales: concepts, order, transfer, and estimation. Students approached tasks conceptually by building on their

mental images of fractions, whereas students using the other curricula focused on standard and rote procedures for solving fraction tasks.

3. Driscoll discusses these two features of students' work with patterns and their relationship to algebraic thinking. Extended work with patterns can help students to learn about functional relationships (a fundamental concept of algebra). Such experiences also help students to look beyond a perceived pattern to find general rules that always work. The thinking process of generalization is important in all areas of mathematics.

Chapter

3

Making Writing a Seamless
Part of Learning Mathematics

In previous chapters some basic ideas about writing and mathematics have been developed along with some suggestions and strategies to assist in constructing writing experiences for mathematics students. This chapter continues the development of those ideas by emphasizing how writing can become a seamless part of mathematical learning. What exactly do we mean by this? Writing in mathematics gives students an opportunity to take ownership of the concepts and ideas being studied in the classroom. Writing is a means of using language to form meaning and build understanding. Students need to see writing in mathematics as an essential tool for helping them to better understand concepts, ideas, procedures, and processes. To be effective, writing cannot be perceived merely as an add-on to the regular routine of the mathematics classroom.

The goal of this chapter is to provide some ideas about how writing can become an instrumental part of the mathematics repertoire. Key ideas will assist in planning classrooms in which writing and mathematics go hand in hand to develop and extend students' mathematical literacy. The classrooms in which writing is supported are also classrooms in which communication is valued and encouraged. Throughout this chapter, a broad framework for communication will be developed because it is within such a framework that writing becomes a seamless part of the process of learning mathematics. It is within this framework that writing-to-learn in mathematics can flourish and provide the types of learning results that clearly demonstrate students' progress in developing mathematical literacy.

Planning for a Safe Environment

An important element that requires careful consideration is the classroom environment (Turner et al., 2002; Yackel, 2000). This is particularly important when new ideas and strategies, such as writing as part of the mathematics curriculum, are becoming part of the learning landscape. The type of learning environment that is established in the classroom is very important, and that environment should support and encourage all forms of communication, especially written communication. Although classrooms are unique and individual, there are some characteristics of classrooms that support and encourage mathematical inquiry, and it is those types of classrooms in which writing and other forms of communication become an expectation. The five characteristics described below constitute a core set of principles that is essential if mathematics classrooms are to respect ideas and thoughts and expect good mathematical communication.

A Safe Atmosphere for the Exchange of Ideas

In mathematics, students are accustomed to giving numerical and one- or two-word answers, and in many classrooms students know that if a wrong answer is given the teacher will quickly call on another student until the correct response is given. In classrooms where students are expected to elaborate on their thinking and exchange ideas, there may be a heightened sense of vulnerability. Students must feel that their ideas are valued and that they have something meaningful to contribute.

This holds true for written as well as oral communication. A classroom environment must be established so that students feel empowered to share their ideas. Review the Questions for Building Mathematical Understanding that were presented in Table 2-3. These and the other techniques and strategies throughout this book provide tools for engaging students in reflective thinking about mathematics. This is the first step in establishing a safe environment. Questioning that requires reflective thinking and sharing of ideas must be part of the learning environment. This idea is elaborated on later in this chapter in a discussion of the nature of tasks. There are three levels at which the teacher must consider how to set the stage for promoting a safe atmosphere for the exchange of ideas: whole-class discussions, small groups, and paired exchanges between students or between student and teacher.

In whole-class discussions, the teacher must model the type of communication that is valued and expected. Students will benefit from the teacher doing a role-play that focuses on "When I ask for you to explain your thinking, this is what I am expecting." Another method for establishing such expectations is to point out when good communication takes place. For example, if an interchange between students or between the teacher and a student demonstrates the qualities of good mathematical communication, take a few minutes to let the class know that the interchange was valuable, and note two or three things that made it so. Create a safe environment by encouraging students to share ideas. Listen carefully to what students are saying. If contributions lack substance, listen for a key word or idea from the student, then use that key word or idea to further the discussion.

Benefit can be realized when the teacher picks up on and probes an incorrect or incomplete response (NCTM, 2000).[1] In an atmosphere in which misconceptions and errors are examined, students learn to deal appropriately with their evolving mathematical thinking. Never allow a student to make embarrassing or negative comments about the contribution of another student. Follow the same procedures when observing exchanges between students during group or paired situations. If whole-class settings promote a safe environment, it is easy to extend those considerations and expectations to a small-group setting. The following vignette shows these principles in practice in a fifth-grade mathematics classroom:

Teacher: Yan says that when you multiply two fractions, the answer will always be smaller. Let's think about that. Renee, what happens when I multiply two whole numbers?

Renee: Ummm . . .

Teacher: Consider 2 and 4, for example.

Renee: You get 8.

Teacher: Is that smaller or larger than the numbers you're multiplying? Lamont?

Lamont: It is larger than both 2 and 4.

Teacher: Good. How does that compare with what Yan is saying?

Tina: It's backwards.

Teacher: What do you mean?

Tina: Well, Yan is saying the answer is smaller.

Teacher: Who can give us an example of what Yan is saying?

(Several students raise their hands.)

Teacher: Chris?

Chris: $1/2$ times $1/3$ is $1/6$. $1/6$ is smaller.

Teacher: Can anyone think of an example when this isn't true?

(Several minutes go by as students think and try combinations on their papers. Then a student raises her hand.)

Darlene: $2/3$ times $2/3$ is $2/3$. It's the same. Not bigger or smaller.

Teacher: Who agrees with Darlene?

Ralph: Shouldn't the answer be $4/9$? How did you get $2/3$?

Darlene: I—Oops! I got $4/6$. I added the bottoms.

Teacher: Let's think about why multiplying two fractions gives you a product smaller than the two numbers.

(Teacher goes to the board and draws a circle.)

Teacher: Let's imagine this is a pizza. I'll shade $1/2$. That's all I have left. Now, I want to give you $1/2$ of what I have. How much of a whole pizza will that be?

Yan: That's $1/4$ of a pizza. It's smaller than $1/2$.

Teacher: Good. If I have part of something and give someone part of it, will they ever get more than I started with?

(Class echoes with group no.*)*

Teacher: So, we've done some serious thinking about what it means to multiply two fractions. Now I want you to draw me another example with a rectangle. Be sure to write the multiplication problem. Then tell me why you think Yan makes sense.

Mutual Trust and Respect

Trust and respect might be considered by-products of an environment in which students feel safe to share ideas. Respect and trust are essential in mathematics classrooms in which learning takes place through an exchange of ideas. Once again, teachers should model appropriate behaviors for their students. Following students' questions and building on students' ideas and responses is one way to develop trust and respect in classroom interactions. Students must perceive that ideas and contributions are important and that everyone has something valuable to say. This is not always easy, and teachers have to be sensitive to goals and classroom time constraints. A teacher can, however, acknowledge shared ideas while letting the class know that time constraints prohibit further exploration of those ideas.

Teachers must keep class interactions focused while showing respect for students' contributions. It is also helpful to know students' strengths and weaknesses. This is especially important if the teacher knows that a student who struggles somewhat is doing well with a particular concept. This is a good time to engage the student more in classroom sharing. Students should come to realize that the teacher is motivated to understand their thinking rather than merely looking for the correct answer. Differences in thinking and different approaches have to be valued. In classrooms where students are routinely asked to share multiple methods, the climate is one in which differences are expected and valued. In such environments students will come to appreciate the process of considering the thinking of others without becoming defensive or fearful (Hiebert et al., 1997; Stepanek, 2000).

A Focus on Ideas Instead of Individuals

Communication, both written and oral, should be viewed as a set of actions that promotes understanding instead of being a mere outlet for sharing information. Moffett and Wagner (1992) relate that in vibrant communication exchanges, ideas are picked up and developed through substantiating, qualifying, elaborating, building on, amending, and varying the ideas that are communicated.

Furthermore, experiences will help students to anticipate the level of engagement and the types of questions that will be asked, and they will begin to supply more information before the teacher or other students prompt them. One way of promoting this process is to repeat, or ask a student to repeat, what someone has shared. This helps to develop listening skills and lets students know that what is being said is important. Focus on the meaning of the mathematics. Emphasize the key concepts, rules, definitions, and procedures that students are using. When errors occur, focus on what went wrong mathematically with the thinking. Focusing on analyzing errors when they occur helps students to understand that ideas, not just answers, are important. Having students write what they learn from an exchange or reviewing an error is a good way to reinforce the importance of the ideas and the thinking of others.

Tasks That Promote Inquiry and Investigation

Tasks that engage students in meaningful exploration of important mathematics are important elements in this vision of school mathematics. Rich tasks develop a different thinking about mathematics than the traditional problem sets that characterize students' mathematical activity.

First, rich tasks focus on the process of *doing* mathematics instead of the final answer. The end product is important; however, it is students' thinking to arrive at that solution that has the potential to transform the energy of the mathematics classroom. Rich tasks may not always have a single answer but may have multiple appropriate solutions.

Second, rich tasks provide opportunities for students to justify and reason about the mathematics involved. Such experiences help students to develop a deeper conceptual understanding of important mathematics as they are engaged in communicating about the mathematical principles involved in their investigation.

Third, rich tasks involve multiple mathematics concepts and ideas that require the application of various mathematics processes. This is important to remember in planning for such levels of engagement. Teachers often initially think that such tasks are not efficient because they require greater segments of time to complete; however, the tasks require a much more sophisticated use of mathematics, develop multiple reasoning and problem-solving strategies, and involve a greater number of important mathematics concepts than do typical problems. There is growing evidence that this type of curriculum has a positive impact on student performance in mathematics (Senk & Thompson, 2003).

Physical Environmental Considerations That Encourage Communication

Physical environments send a message about what is important in the classroom. One factor in planning for vibrant learning environments is the arrangement of desks. To promote collaboration in small groups, cluster the desks or put students around tables. Four desks can be arranged so that two desks face two other desks. This allows students to work together, and it saves times in rearranging desks for peer and group activities. If classroom discussions are frequent, desks might be arranged in a U-shape or a circle.

Teachers may initially feel uncomfortable allowing students to face each other and may have concerns about management issues. Creating clear expectations about when it is appropriate to talk is crucial. Teachers who routinely use this arrangement indicate that management issues can be dealt with quickly and that arrangements allowing students to collaborate make it easier to engage more students in classroom activities. Students benefit from working and talking together about the mathematics being studied.

In addition to the arrangement of desks, the classroom should contain materials that support student engagement. Bulletin boards can be used to display student work; tables, charts, and other organizers of material being studied; and other information relative to the topic. Commercial materials are attractive, but student materials and materials that can be altered communicate that learning is ongoing and that students' ideas are valued. Word walls displaying important terms, including graphics and examples, are another way to promote the importance of mathematical communication. Student-generated materials communicate the importance of student ideas and contributions to learning.

Focusing on Communication in the Mathematics Classroom

Written communication is only one tool, albeit a significant one, for extending students' learning in mathematics. Speaking and listening also play an important role in shaping students' learning experiences. Another consideration in a language-rich mathematics environment is attention to students' reading and comprehension. Below are some ideas that show how these factors can be brought together to provide a rich and vibrant learning environment that makes communication part of the classroom.

Listening

There are important considerations about students' listening in mathematics that teachers should be aware of when planning for instruction that promotes communication, including written forms. Listening is active. Dewey (1927) said that hearing is participation. Listening requires active engagement of one's thinking so that information can be understood, interpreted, and processed.

Although teachers might not focus on developing listening skills, understanding the importance of listening and reinforcing good listening practices is something that can be done as a routine part of teaching mathematics. Given the amount of information in mathematics classrooms that is transmitted verbally by the teacher and other students, listening well is essential in promoting mathematical understanding.

What are important listening skills? Many state standards frameworks include listening as part of the language arts curriculum. Among the skills identified are paraphrasing, summarizing, and asking questions for elaboration or clarification. Listening involves connecting to previous ideas and building on the information being presented. Many of the ideas about questioning and writing presented in other chapters support the development of listening. In fact, writing in mathematics supports the type of thinking and reflecting that is indicative of active listening. Listening is extremely important if students are to think about the teacher's and peers' ideas and how that information changes their own mathematical understanding. Research indicates that effective students repeat one another's statements more frequently (Stacy & Gooding, 1998). Listening carefully is essential if students are to use the language of others to support and extend their thinking about mathematics.

How, specifically, can teachers support the development of students' listening behaviors? The follow suggestions focus on behaviors that directly help students to connect and build on the ideas being presented in class:

1. Encourage students to paraphrase key ideas and information. Writing activities frequently require students to paraphrase information. Focus on helping students to paraphrase information effectively. Writing and listening in this regard become complementary tools.

2. Expect students to summarize information. Although this is an excellent writing focus, students benefit from observing this in action. Ask students to summarize key ideas, steps, or concepts as part of class. When students are working in pairs or groups, ask them to stop and summarize what has been done so far, their understanding of the task, or the mathematics that supports their work.

3. Help students to ask good questions. Teachers who model good questions can expect that students will begin to use those types of questions. If students ask vague or confusing questions, help them to restate their questions. Chapter 2 provides a good framework for the types of questions that promote mathematical inquiry and require students to listen and think about information.

Speaking

Speaking receives more explicit attention in the curriculum than listening, but the interrelatedness of the two warrants specific attention to each. A growing body of research shows that talking and discussing are related to students' level of learning (Applebee et al., 2003; Hiebert & Wearne, 1992; Rivard & Straw, 2000). Wood (1998) describes two patterns of communication in mathematics classrooms. The *funnel pattern* is characterized by telling students correct procedures or answers and corresponds to surface-level communication. The *focus pattern* is characterized by students thinking about mathematics, investigating, and discussing their ideas with others. Although students are somewhat at risk in focusing because their thinking is subject to public evaluation, they realize that they are part of a community in which clarification and justification are expected. Such environments focus students' attention and enable the teacher to guide as students give explanations and reasons for their mathematical thinking.

The quality of speaking and thinking that occurs in mathematics classrooms is related to the level of written communication that students construct. Chapter 2 provided some suggestions to guide teachers in constructing questions that promote deep mathematical thinking. These questions are an appropriate framework for both written and oral communication. As teachers plan for mathematics lessons, some thought should be given to how and in what forms communication will be fostered in the lesson. *Professional Standards for Teaching Mathematics* (NCTM, 1991) describes how teachers can make plans for effective classroom discourse: pose questions and provide tasks that elicit, engage, and challenge students; listen carefully to the thinking of students; ask students to justify and clarify their ideas (orally and in writing); decide what to pursue in depth from among the ideas students bring to discussions; decide when and in what ways mathematical notation and language should be connected to students' ideas; decide when to give information and details, when to clarify, when to model, when to lead, and when to allow students to struggle with an idea, a problem, or a concept; and monitor discussions and decide when and how to encourage participation. This is a lot to consider; however, the ideas presented throughout this book provide strategies and information to guide that decision-making process.

Spoken language is a key part of students' actions when working in groups. Elaboration is a key feature of effective peer interaction. Research shows that students who explain to their peers and give extended answers show higher achievement than others in the group (Webb, 1991). Facilitating group interactions so that the processing is effective requires careful attention and close monitoring. As the teacher plans for instruction, thought should be given to the nature of the task to support mathematical communication, how the task can be set up to maximize student engagement, and possible questions and information that will help students to discuss significant mathematical concepts and ideas. Knowledge of the characteristics of effective group communication can help when planning for collaborative work. Stacey and Gooding (1998) studied groups working on division concepts. They found that effective groups did the following:

- Talked more, with the talk containing more mathematical content
- Explicitly discussed the main mathematical idea of the task
- Worked cooperatively by reading statements from text materials and repeating one another's statements
- Proposed ideas, gave explanations that included mathematical evidence, and refocused discussion
- Responded to questions of others

Students in effective groups exhibited these behaviors more frequently than groups that were not effective in the tasks. Although mistakes were made in the mathematical talk, talking seemed to provide a way of exposing misconceptions and providing an interactive context for dealing with them. The characteristics of effective group processing provide some criteria that can guide teachers in facilitating group communication.

Reading

Reading, though frequently not stressed in mathematics teaching, is imperative in promoting mathematical learning and contributing to successful written communication. Writing-to-learn in mathematics is intrinsically related to students' reading and rereading their own and others' written texts as important mathematical ideas and concepts are refined and explained. Full attention to reading is beyond the scope of this book, but there are basic ideas about reading that will assist teachers in planning useful writing activities. When students are going to encounter text in their mathematical work, the purpose for reading and working with the text are important considerations. Borasi & Siegel (2000) identify three reasons for students to read in mathematics: to learn from the text, to support and enhance mathematical inquiry, and to negotiate a learning community.

Learning from the text is the most apparent. Besides learning technical information, students can understand the big ideas in mathematics through this activity. The meanings that are developed from the texts should become part of the interactive relationship among reading, writing, listening, and speaking. When a lesson requires students to read a text, the teacher should identify the meaning that students should construct from the text and how that meaning relates to the big ideas in mathematics. By identifying these features, teachers can monitor and aid students in reading and comprehending the text with specific outcomes in mind.

In the second purpose of reading in mathematics, to support and enhance mathematical inquiry, students may read a text to clarify ideas and conjectures, identify tasks and decisions, gather resources and models for a problem, and review and revise thinking about mathematics. The text as well as supplementary resources should be considered, with some thought as to how those materials can be used capably by students. Direction and modeling may be necessary to help students begin to develop skills in using available resources, including their mathematics textbook.

In the third purpose of reading, to negotiate a learning community, this community builds on the idea of inquiry and supports the notion of making mathematics a public endeavor instead of a private and isolated learning process. Provide opportunities for students to collectively make sense of the text, particularly when the text to be used may be conceptually dense. Reading aloud, constructing lists of ideas, and following up with discussion make it easier for students to comprehend the text and develop skills that will assist them in the future.

Activity

The activity in Table 3-1 combines the four communication modes that we've emphasized in this chapter. The context is helping students to learn about numbers, but the activity is easily adaptable to other topics. Teachers write clues on a series of four cards to be read sequentially. One student reads the clue and another student comes up with a response from the clue and writes a justification to support the response. At the end, the partner can agree or disagree with the conclusion. If the partner disagrees, he or she can provide another response but must be able to justify the mathematics behind the new answer. The students then switch roles. Teachers might devise a point system if students are interested in making this activity into a game.

Table 3-1.   Communication Activity

Clue	Response	Justification
The number is smaller than the number that, when squared, will result in 10,000.	Must be less than 100.	100 multiplied by 100 is 10,000.
The number is larger than 2^4.	Number must be between 16 and 100.	2^4 is 2 x 2 x 2 x 2 or 16.
The number is a multiple of 15.	The number must be 30, 45, 60, 75, or 90.	Multiples are answers from the times table. For 15 that is 30, then 45, then 60, then 75, then 90.
The number is divisible by 9 but not by 10.	The number is 45.	45 and 90 are divisible by 9. 90 can be divided by 10, but 45 can't.

Summary

This chapter provided ideas that link writing with listening, speaking, and reading. Communication modes do not develop independently of one another, and this is no different in the mathematics classroom. What does it mean for writing to be a seamless part of the mathematics classroom? The Hyperdictionary (Webnox, 2003) defines *seamless* as "perfectly consistent and coherent." In designing mathematics lessons in which writing is a consistent and coherent part of teaching and learning, attention should be given to other modes of communication. Lindquist and Elliott (1996) argue that individuals learn language by talking, listening, reading, and writing, in the same way that mathematics is learned.

Classrooms in which communication can be fostered require a safe and vibrant atmosphere for the exchange of ideas, mutual trust and respect, a focus on ideas instead of individuals, tasks that promote inquiry and investigation, and physical environmental considerations that encourage communication. In this type of environment, teachers can plan activities and lessons that promote mathematical communication. The information in this chapter on listening, speaking, and reading provide key design considerations that combine with writing to create the types of learning communities in which mathematical ideas are developed and exchanged. These learning communities create rich language environments that sustain effective mathematics learning and assist students as they develop mathematical literacy.

Note

1. The NCTM standards provides examples of classroom exchanges that show what communication should look like in the mathematics classroom. It is recognized that classroom discussion should advance the goals of the lesson. The discussion in the standards gives insight into practices that promote the type of classroom environments in which students are actively engaged in building mathematical understanding.

Part

II

Implementing

Chapter

4

Promoting Standards and Communicating Expectations

Too frequently, recommendations for writing in mathematics appear to be made with little indication that such communicative processes have to be developed. Good writing in mathematics doesn't just happen; it has to be nurtured and developed. Students must develop a sense of what constitutes good writing in mathematics. Students should not develop an impression that their mathematical writing is background work with little direct connection with their mathematical learning but should see their writing as directly linked to their mathematical study.

The first three chapters focused on explicit consideration of writing as part of the planning process for mathematics learning. The next three chapters focus on implementation issues that will assist the teacher as writing in mathematics is put into practice. Our first concern in this regard is to discuss how standards and expectations for good writing are communicated in the classroom. This chapter includes a discussion on why expectations are important, what constitutes good writing—especially in mathematics teaching and learning—and offers some suggestions on how teachers can help students to develop a sense of what is good mathematical writing. These are very important initial steps that set the stage for continued progress and growth in students' mathematical writing and consequently in their mathematical thinking.

Expectations and Student Achievement

Some basic information about the relationship between expectations and student achievement is in order before the discussion continues on how to develop clear and high expectations for writing in mathematics. There is empirical evidence that high expectations for student achievement is one of the school-level factors that contributes to school effectiveness (Marzano, 2000). In general, high expectations are communicated as a goal that clearly articulates that academic achievement is of primary importance and that all students should exceed academically. Although high expectations are a schoolwide component of effective schools, the teacher is a primary agent in developing this type of climate in the classroom and contributing to the overall school climate. The mathematics classroom provides a critical space in which students come to realize classroom expectations as well as the broader expectations of the larger school community. Writing in mathematics gives teachers an influential context in which to send a message about what it means to learn and understand mathematics. Clear expectations about understanding mathematics and the role of communication as a learning tool are expressed when teachers communicate clear ideas and goals for writing in mathematics. Students must understand and internalize these expectations in order to be successful, especially since most will not possess clear guidelines about writing in mathematics.

What Is Good Mathematical Writing?

Students may arrive in mathematics without well-developed writing skills and without a real sense of what makes writing good (in any discipline). Getting individuals to decide on the characteristics of good writing might prove difficult. The goal here is not to drag mathematics teachers into this debate but to provide some common principles that will help teachers to implement a sound and solid writing-to-learn program in their instruction. The following are some elements that writing specialists would agree are indicative of good writing:

1. The writing expresses a clear sense of purpose. It is done with a purpose that is evident in the final product.
2. The structure and development provide details, arguments, justifications, and assertions that lead to a conclusion.

3. Information and ideas are conveyed in a precise and concise manner.

4. Basic grammar and mechanics are evident.

These four components are basic beginning points that can help students to understand the expectations for writing in mathematics. Later these will be further developed and contextualized in mathematics. Mathematics teachers may consider working with language arts teachers in reviewing these four basic components as part of language arts instruction. This would further emphasize the connections between language and mathematics. The language arts teacher may emphasize other basic principles. As the mathematics teacher, you can decide to emphasize others or focus on these four. Teachers find that these four provide an excellent entry point for engaging students in thinking about the elements of good writing and that they are crucial in shaping some common understanding about what is expected from writing in mathematics.

The most prevalent framework used in considering the quality of written work includes six points. The four elements presented above provide a more concise system for mathematics teachers to use when considering the quality of writing. The four elements incorporate the six points used in many language arts programs. A comparison of the two ways of looking at the characteristics of good writing (Table 4-1) demonstrates that the more concise four-element system retains the essential components while incorporating the basic intent and spirit of the six-point model.

Without compromising the strength of the six-trait model, *ideas & content* and *organization* are combined in the four elements in considering how the writing's structure and development provide details, arguments, justifications, and assertions that lead to a conclusion. *Voice* and purpose of writing accomplish the same goal of reflecting on why the writing was done and for whom. *Word choice* and *sentence fluency* can be considered through an analysis of how information and ideas are conveyed, with an emphasis on their precision and conciseness. *Conventions* is a broad descriptor that includes various language mechanics and grammar. The six-trait model is an excellent framework; however, the objective is to provide a usable and comprehensive model for mathematics teachers that doesn't require substantive training in language arts theory and pedagogy. Emphasizing four elements of good writing accomplishes that objective. Some elementary and middle school teachers may have such language arts backgrounds and can decide to revise or extend these ideas to address their instructional goals.

Table 4-1.   Comparison of Six Traits and Four Elements

Six Trait	Description	4-Elements System
Ideas & Content	Ideas are clear and focused. Thoughts are well developed with appropriate details.	The structure and development provide details, arguments, justifications, and assertions that lead to a conclusion.
Organization	Ideas flow from one point to the next. The beginning and ending are strong.	
Voice	The style is interesting and appropriate for the audience as well as the topic.	The writing expresses a clear sense of purpose. It is done with a purpose that is evident in the final product.
Word Choice	Words convey precise and clear meaning and tone.	Information and ideas are conveyed in a precise and concise manner.
Sentence Fluency	Sentences flow smoothly and are varied in structure.	
Conventions	Good mechanics such as spelling, grammar, punctuation, and capitalization are consistent.	Basic grammar and mechanics are evident.

Applying the Four Elements

The following example applies these four elements to a writing exercise completed by a fifth-grade student after a series of lessons on comparing fractions. This task might also be appropriate for elementary and middle school students. Teachers should consider what they would like students to demonstrate through mathematical writing, because different mathematical approaches are likely to be offered by students. Although several approaches will be mathematically sound, the teacher should use writing to help students understand the strengths and weaknesses of various methods. Teachers should show respect and value various approaches while also promoting good mathematical thinking.

In the task shown in Figure 4-1, the teacher's goal was for students to use some number sense related to benchmarks for fractions. One of the lessons in the unit had included a great deal of thinking and talking about how $^1/_4$, $^1/_3$, $^1/_2$, $^2/_3$, $^3/_4$, and 1 could be used as markers when comparing fractions. The task engaged students in comparing three fractions to determine their order from smallest to largest: $^5/_{10}$, $^5/_3$, and $^5/_6$.

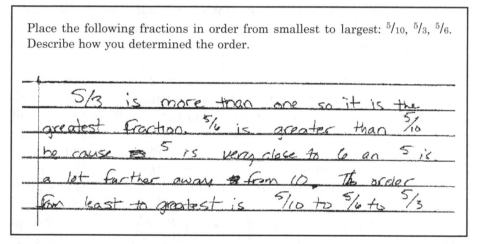

Place the following fractions in order from smallest to largest: $^5/_{10}$, $^5/_3$, $^5/_6$. Describe how you determined the order.

> 5/3 is more than one so it is the greatest fraction. 5/6 is greater than 5/10 be cause 5 is very close to 6 an 5 is a lot farther away from 10. The order from least to greatest is 5/10 to 5/6 to 5/3

Figure 4-1. Fraction Exercise

Our discussion will begin with an analysis of this student's work using the four elements of good writing. The student's response met the teacher's expectations for the task. Later in the chapter this task will be revisited, with a discussion on how the teacher responded to other students' responses.

Element 1: The writing expresses a clear sense of purpose. It is done with a purpose that is evident in the final product. The student could have done a better job stating the goal of the task instead of going immediately into a discussion of his thinking. Nevertheless, the writing reveals that the student's purpose was to explain how he would order certain fractions. The final answer provides a clear indicator of the purpose of the writing. In stating that the order from least to greatest is $^5/_{10}$, $^5/_6$, and $^5/_3$, the student is showing that he understood and could react to the purpose of the writing.

Element 2: The structure and development provide details, arguments, justifications, and assertions that lead to a conclusion. The student did not perform in this element as well as the teacher would have liked. She therefore engaged the student in discussing how he could have provided more detail about his answers. For example, the teacher asked the student to tell how he knew $^5/_3$ is greater than 1. She also wasn't convinced that the student could justify his approach of comparing the distance of the numerator from the denominator. She asked him to think about this some more and see if he could mathematically justify this approach. (The student did later point out that because the numerators were the same, this approach would be valid because "5 would be the number of parts out of the whole.") Despite these points for improvement, the teacher thought that the student performed well on providing detail. There was a justification for how he determined the rank of each of the fractions, and those justifications were grounded in sound mathematical reasoning.

Element 3: Information and ideas are conveyed in a precise and concise manner. The student's response was written in a concise fashion. There were no statements that did not contribute to the development of the answer. The teacher would have preferred the use of more precise language, such as *numerator* and *denominator,* but there were no instances in which terms were used inappropriately.

Element 4: Basic grammar and mechanics are evident. The teacher wants to promote good use of grammar and mechanics but acknowledges that she doesn't want to become an English teacher. She wants students to feel free to write their ideas without worrying excessively about grammar and mechanics. She points out common errors that she picks up while reviewing the students' work, however, and she shares these with the class, noting that if there are several obvious mistakes, the response is not an excellent piece of writing. She frequently asks students to correct their errors. Other teachers may deal differently with this issue, but this teacher believed that her instructional goals were best met by not overemphasizing mechanics in writing. She preferred to point out errors without penalizing the student. Elementary teachers must consider their students' development level as writers and continue to adjust expectations as students become more refined writers. Some writing that is done in mathematics isn't a finished product, and many teachers choose to emphasize content and rich descriptions over mechanics. These issues and others will be explored in more detail in the chapters dealing with assessment.

This student's writing measures up well to each of the four elements. Understanding the basic characteristics of how these four components relate to good writing is essential when beginning to implement writing in mathematics. Students should be made aware of the qualities that are acceptable for the written assignments. Teachers will have to repeat this type of discussion if a writing task is significantly different from others that have been done in the class. For example, a formal report would require some additional work in helping students to understand how the four elements apply in that type of writing. The teacher in this classroom used this particular student's writing as a strong illustration of each of the four elements. This is part of an effective trajectory for helping students to develop a clear sense of expectations for good writing in mathematics. This trajectory is depicted in Figure 4-2.

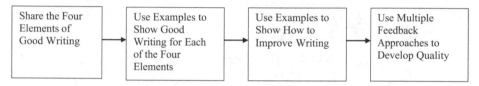

Figure 4-2. Model for Communicating Writing Expectations

The discussion thus far has focused on the first two parts of this model. Students need a basic overview of the teacher's expectations about good writing. Going over the four elements is a good way to give students some basic ideas to guide their thinking about writing. These ideas should be grounded in concrete examples. The second aspect of this model is to show students what good writing looks like for each of the four elements. This is vital if students are to develop a clear understanding of the form of writing.

Using Examples to Help Students Improve Writing

Students need time and experience to understand the qualities of good mathematical writing. The third aspect of the model for developing this understanding is to use examples of student work to help students improve their writing. This topic will be revisited later when assessment is discussed more thoroughly. At this time, the discussion will focus on how examples of students' writing can promote clear guidelines about expectations for writing in mathematics. The task in which students were asked to describe how they would order three fractions from smallest to greatest will be used in this discussion. Keep in mind that this is a first step in implementing an effective writing-to-learn program in mathematics. This is part of a comprehensive and interrelated framework that involves planning, implementing, and assessing.

It is sometimes helpful to identify a few things that would focus the writing and make it more acceptable. The student (Figure 4-3) did answer the question and demonstrates some understanding of the nature of fractions; however, there is not enough explanation or description to justify the approach. She shows that she understands that 5/3 has to be the largest because 5 (the numerator) is bigger than 3 (the denominator).

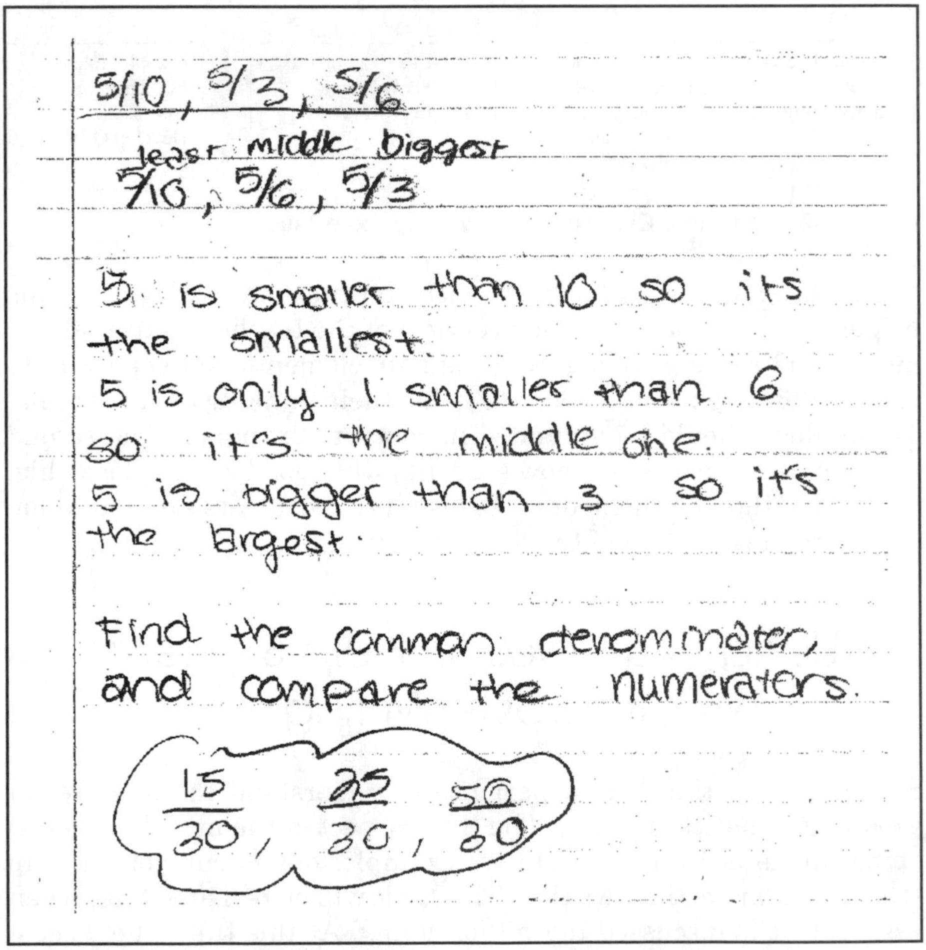
5/10, 5/3, 5/6

least middle biggest

5/10, 5/6, 5/3

5 is smaller than 10 so its the smallest.

5 is only 1 smaller than 6 so it's the middle one.

5 is bigger than 3 so it's the largest.

Find the comman denominater, and compare the numeraters.

15/30, 25/30, 50/30

Figure 4-3. Focus on Improving Student Response—First Example

Nevertheless, the response leaves too much to interpretation. What is meant by "compare the numerators"? The approach is similar to the one described previously, but there aren't clear details and arguments to support assumptions (element 2).

What advice could be given to the student? First, the good ideas should be valued. The student's approach is insightful and does suggest that she understands how the fractions compare to 1. For example, she talks about 5 being only 1 smaller than 6, which seems to indicate that it is close to 1. How could the student clarify this response? She should be encouraged to explain why 5 being only 1 smaller than 6 is mathematically meaningful. She isn't using mathematical justification and reasoning to support her approach.

A second item to focus on would be the addition of the alternative method of rewriting the fractions with common denominators. Although this demonstrates flexibility in approach, the writing should be more focused. Students should be encouraged to describe one method well. Encourage students to think, "What mathematical reasoning can I use to support what I'm doing?" For younger students this might best be developed by asking them to tell why or how something works.

Another point is to encourage the use of mathematical language. Students need opportunities and support for using mathematical vocabulary. In some cases, the teacher might want to ask students to use particular words in their responses. In this example, students could have been asked to use *numerator* and *denominator* in their responses.

Overall, this student's work was considered to be a good response to the problem, especially because the students were still novices in writing in mathematics.

Consider a second example (Figure 4-4). This one raises some serious questions. The student uses a technique that should lead her to a correct answer.

What did this student do that could serve as a springboard for promoting a satisfactory response? The student is using an approach

list the fractions in order by dimater. Going greatest to least. 5/10, 5/6, 5/3. Thats the way I would solve the problem in this case.

(5/10, 5/3 5/6) are the fractions. (0.5, 1.6, 0.83)

devide the numaratr by the denomator see what you get. Than write out the fractions going least to greatest.

Figure 4-4. Focus on Improving Student Response—Second Example

that may not be the most efficient but can be used to order the fractions. She provides some detail to support the actions taken. She describes how she changed the fractions to decimals. She states an intermediate goal, to write out the fractions from least to greatest. This is an excellent starting point from which to launch a discussion about extending and improving the response. This goal also provides a recap of the purpose of the writing, as indicated in element 1. Many teachers do not stress including a goal for writing because the students' work is frequently accompanied by a problem or task, which serves as the goal. Sometimes, however, the task or problem is not on the student's paper, and stating a goal for the writing task thus becomes important.

Students should also understand misstatements and omissions. A useful way of doing this is to illustrate with real examples the types of problems that result in a piece of writing not receiving a high rating. In this example, an obvious problem is that the student did not continue with the process that she described. This refers to element 2: She did not provide details of thinking and actions that lead to a conclusion. After calculating the decimals, the student did not order them and provide a final answer.

There are some notable problems with element 3 as well. The student does not identify the precise decimal representations of $^5/_3$ and $^5/_6$ ($^5/_3$ = 1.666 . . . = 1.67 and $^5/_6$ = 0.8333 . . . = 0.83). Because technology provides students with a tool for quickly completing computations, the teacher should expect a certain level of precision in how the results of those computations are recorded. The student should have indicated that 1.6 and 0.83 are repeating decimals. The level of precision is important to point out so that the student is careful in other contexts where precision can affect the answer.

Another problem, which relates to both elements 2 and 3, is the student's ordering of the fractions by their denominators as an initial step. This step was not related to the student's solution process. The student should have addressed that this action did not contribute to finding a solution. When students change their thinking and redirect their actions, they should be encouraged to acknowledge that in their writing by stating that the approach wasn't successful and that something else was done. Encourage them to provide some explanation of why the approach wasn't right. This helps students to learn from their initial thinking by reflecting on the mathematics related to their work.

In reference to element 4, there are misspelled words that the teacher should point out: *dimater, gratest, devide, numarotr, denomator,* and *than* for *then* are not acceptable. *Divide, numerator,* and *denominator*, in particular, are important and basic mathematical terms. In such cases students should be encouraged to correct major spelling problems.

The third example (Figure 4-5) demonstrates a minimal response to the task and provides a context for discussing how to encourage students who are reluctant writers to engage more fully in the writing process.

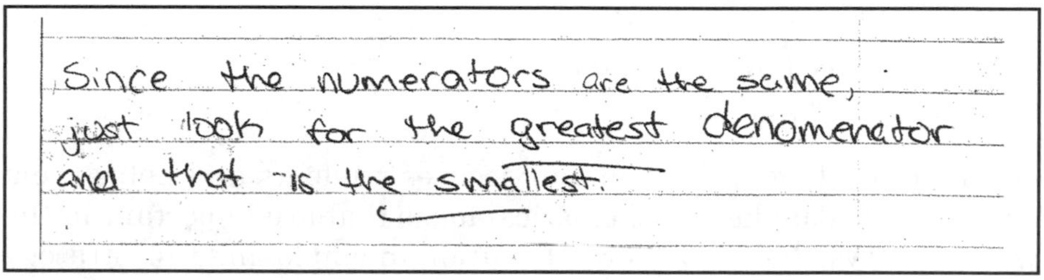

Since the numerators are the same, just look for the greatest denomenator and that is the smallest.

Figure 4-5. Focus on Improving Student Response—Third Example

There is evidence that this student has sound number reasoning skills. She knows that because the numerators are equal, the denominators hold the key to ordering the fractions. Her one sentence implies that if the parts (numerators) are the same, then a larger number of total parts in the whole (denominator) would result in a smaller quantity.

How can such students be encouraged to write convincing details? One possibility would be to ask the student to convince you (the teacher) that this is true—that it will always work—and/or to ask the student to show how she would apply this reasoning. Both are solid procedures for promoting reflective thinking and helping students to extend their writing. Writing convincing arguments employs higher order thinking and develops students' mathematical reasoning skills. Students come to appreciate the power of mathematical justification. Writing also requires students to demonstrate how they are applying concepts, ideas, and processes to particular contexts. Students should show how their thinking applies to the particular tasks—that is, although their writing may refer to more general mathematics and concepts, students should use the numbers in the task to show how they are applying those ideas.

Students might have a limited sense of how to approach such writing exercises, and they might need some structure that helps them to begin to frame an acceptable response. Using students' work to build such a framework helps students to see the examples as not contrived or artificial but emerging from the actual thinking of a peer. The following example shows how a framework or skeleton for writing can provide entry points for many struggling writers while advancing the standards for the quality of writing that will lead to greater mathematical understanding. This skeleton is based on the student response discussed in this section.

> I need to . . .
>
> I notice . . .
>
> This means . . .
>
> Thus I need to . . . because . . .
>
> Therefore, the . . .

This type of mental scaffolding focuses students and helps them as they articulate key mathematical ideas that are important in the writing. Nevertheless, a word of caution in employing this strategy is in order: Care must be taken that students do not think that this is the only format for the response or that the number of sentences is restricted to those indicated in the framework. The framework provides a useful structure that illustrates the application of the four elements. The first and the last sentence each communicate the purpose of the writing. What is it that needs to be done, and what is the conclusion? The structure of the framework encourages students to think about details and supporting ideas. *This means* and *because* are signal words that require the student to stop and reflect on what is going on and provide mathematical reasons to support the actions and ideas. The precision of the framework allows the teacher to model the effective use of mathematical language while also creating an opportunity to stress good mechanics and grammar.

With this framework, the teacher can engage the students in talking about the task. This is an excellent opportunity for the teacher to model effective writing. Using student-generated ideas and language, the teacher can complete the framework with the class. Copy the framework on an overhead projector or some other method by which the class can see the writing unfold. The teacher should think aloud as he or she writes the piece, pausing to ask questions or clarify thinking. The thinking that is part of generating written communication provides a powerful window for students as they refine and develop their own ways of thinking about the mathematics involved in completing exercises and tasks. The following example shows one possible product resulting from using such an approach with a class of fifth graders.

I need to place $^5/_{10}$, $^5/_3$, and $^5/_6$ in order from smallest to largest. *I notice* that the numerators are equal. *This means* that the denominators can be compared to order the fractions. If the numerators are the same, then the number of parts of the whole is the same. The denominators will tell me how many parts the whole has been divided into. *Thus I need to* put the largest denominator first *because* a larger denominator would mean more pieces in the whole—but I will take only 5 of them, so it is a smaller amount of the total. For example, 5 out of 10 pieces would be smaller than 5 out of 6 pieces; 5 out of 3 pieces is all of the pieces and two more. *Therefore, the* answer is $^5/_{10}$, $^5/_6$, and $^5/_3$.

Modeling, talking, and discussing the problem reinforces not only effective listening, speaking, reading, and writing skills but also the power of mathematical thinking. Consider how using this framework facilitates an understanding of the mathematics being considered. The framework shows how thinking can be extended and how mathematical reasoning is incorporated into a response. The example also shows how conceptual understanding of mathematics is promoted through the use of such strategies. Using this strategy offered the teacher a window through which to engage students in thinking about the relationships between denominators and numerators and their role in determining the quantity expressed by a fraction.

Students at early elementary levels will not write extended descriptions of their mathematical thinking as illustrated in the above examples; however, the principles inherent in that discussion will nevertheless apply to all students. The level of writing will differ, but the mathematical engagement of the students will be evident in their work. Figure 4-6 shows how one second-grade student responded to the following problem: The teacher wants to buy cupcakes for her class of 20 students. The cupcakes are sold in boxes of 6 cupcakes each. How many boxes will the teacher need to buy? Will she have any cupcakes left over?

Notice how the student uses diagrams to reason about the problem. Diagrams and pictures are powerful means of communicating about ideas and actions. These diagrams and pictures represent involved and complex thought processes that will later become the basis of students' reasoning and thinking as they extend their communication to using sentences to express their ideas. This foundation is extremely important in developing students' mathematical communication skills. This student demonstrates clearly that she understands how to organize sets of six cupcakes per box. She shows the use of counting to identify the total number of items in the collection. This drawing illustrates how the student thought about the problem. She is providing a visual description and justification for

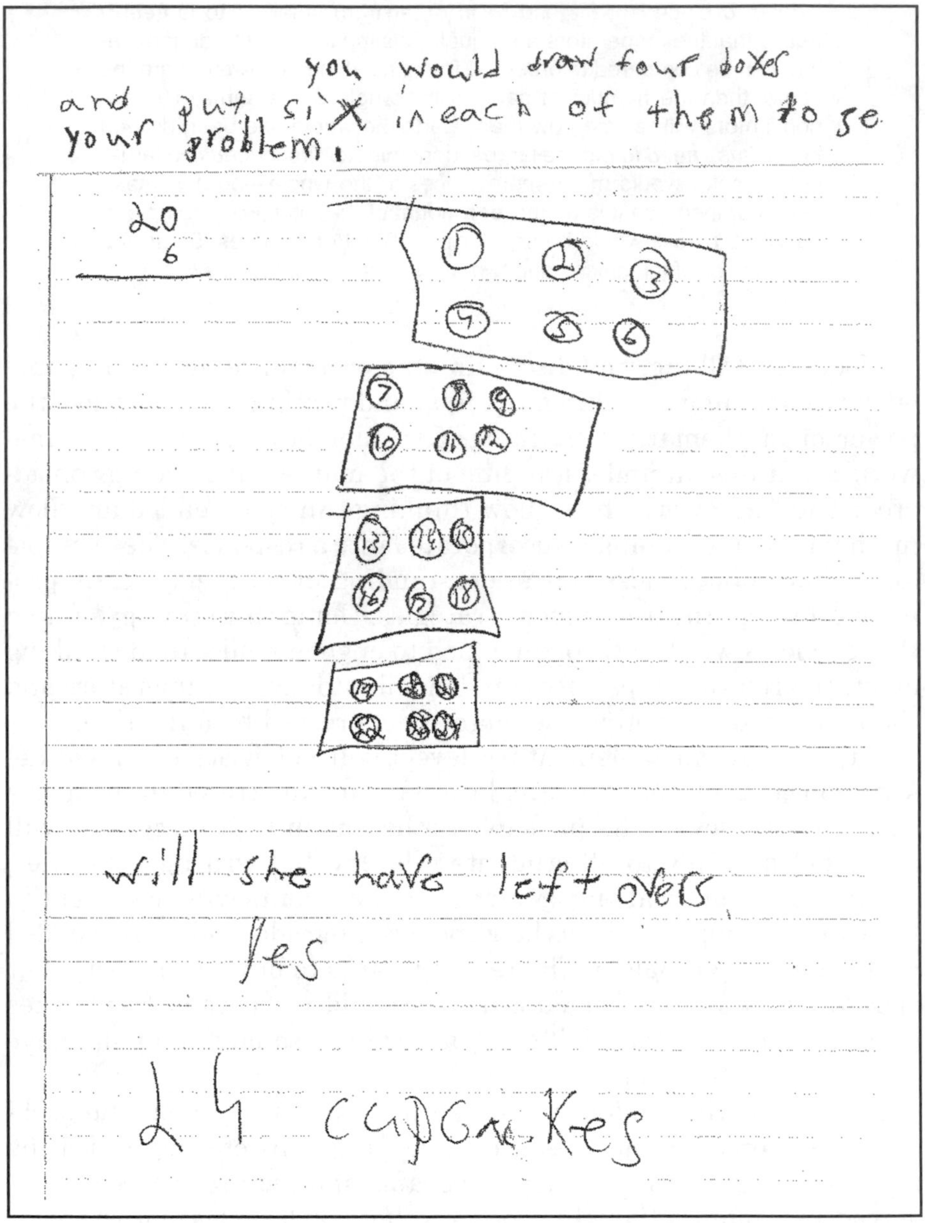

you would draw four boxes
and put six in each of them to se
your problem.

20
6

will she have left overs,
Yes

24 cupcakes

Figure 4-6. Early Elementary Example

what she is doing. Her work supports the four elements. She expresses purpose in her writing when she states the final answer to
the task: Yes, the teacher will have leftovers, and she will need 24
cupcakes. This example, from early in a school year, shows how good
writing can be cultivated in young children. The use of diagrams and
illustrations is a powerful tool in communicating mathematical ideas

to adults. Children should be supported in using such tools to communicate about their thinking; it builds a foundation for expanding the breadth of students' mathematical communication skills and rich mathematical understanding.

Some Strategies for Promoting Standards and Expectations

The discussion thus far has made a case for communicating high expectations and offered some guidelines for conveying high standards for students' writing in mathematics. Some additional strategies that can be used for promoting standards include listing key words, posing questions to guide students, using students' words and thoughts in writing, and using frequent complete-the-statement exercises. These strategies are described below. The focus of the current discussion is on using these strategies to help students develop clear ideas about the how and what of writing in mathematics. These strategies are related to the development of critical thinking skills (Adey, Robertson, & Venville, 2002).

Listing Key Words

One way of helping students to get started with writing and focusing their attention on key ideas is to provide a list of words to be incorporated into the writing task. Vocabulary is an important part of mathematical writing. It embeds rich mathematical concepts in students' thinking about the use and significance of the terms. Providing students with a list of key words and phrases helps them to feel more comfortable in approaching a task. Teachers might consider revisiting this strategy throughout the year as new concepts and ideas are introduced. For example, an eighth-grade lesson on classifying triangles based on their angles could include such terms as *acute, obtuse, right, isosceles,* and *equilateral.* Students could be asked to write a sentence describing each type of triangle.

> Triangles can be named by the types of angles that they have. All angles in *acute* triangles are less than 90°. An *obtuse* triangle has one angle greater than 90°. A *right* triangle has a 90° angle. *Isosceles* triangles have two angles that are the same size. An *isosceles* triangle can also be a *right* triangle, in which case the angles would be 45°, 45°, and 90°. If all the angles in a triangle are the same, it is an *equilateral* triangle, with three 60° angles. The total of all angles in a triangle must be 180°.

Key words help students to know what they should write about the types of triangles. If students aren't ready to write a well-developed response, the teacher might model writing a response with the key words, ask a student to model writing a response, or construct a response with the whole class contributing through discussion. If there are important ideas not given in the response, the teacher can ask students what important information was left out. This scaffolding helps students to develop a cognitive framework that supports good writing.

Posing Questions to Guide Students

Presenting a series of questions can provide students with the necessary framework to construct a good written mathematical response. Novice writers may express difficulty "knowing what to write about." Generating questions that provide a scaffold to direct student thinking is an effective way to help students express their mathematical reasoning. The following first-grade example demonstrates how this might work.

> 7, 10, 13, ____, ____, and ____.
>
> What numbers would you choose?
>
> Do the numbers get larger or smaller?
>
> By how much do the numbers get larger or smaller each time?
>
> In this pattern, what comes after 13?
>
> How did you figure out that number?
>
> What comes next? And last?

Such questions provide a schema for helping students think about the mathematics while also helping to organize their thinking for writing. Such frameworks are also good practice for students who are learning to put their thoughts into words. First-grade students might use phrases such as "grow by 3," "3 more," or "up by 3." In describing what comes after 13 they may provide the sequence 16, 19, 22, 25. Some may write "13 and 3 more" or similar phrases. The questions structure the reasoning that supports the mathematical actions that students will make in completing the pattern.

Students might also be engaged to think about questions that provide a structure for writing about a particular task or problem. This helps to generalize their skills in thinking about communicating mathematically and reveals key information about how they would structure such writing tasks. This information can provide teachers with rich data about students' capabilities, guide mathematics instruction, and emphasize mathematical communication.

Using Students' Words and Thoughts in Writing

This strategy promotes student ownership of the writing process. Students brainstorm ideas related to a problem or task. These ideas are recorded so that they can be used for the writing activity. Initially the teacher should model using the phrases or ideas to write a description. Later, students can use this process working individually or in small groups or pairs. The following fourth-grade example shows how this approach supports mathematical writing.

"A gardener wants to plant 16 plants in the shape of a rectangle. How many different rectangles could she form?" The following ideas were generated by a group of four students working on this problem:

- Each row has to have the same number of plants.
- There could be 4 rows with 4 plants, 8 rows with 2 plants, or 2 rows with 8 plants.
- Those are the same.
- They would look different.

The students' comments contain some important ideas that can be used to model the writing process. This will help the students feel confident that they are ready to use their own thinking to write mathematical descriptions. The following is an example of how the students used the comments to write a group response. The teacher modeled the writing at the direction of the students. The italicized parts were added after the teacher engaged students in more discussion.

If a gardener wants to plant 16 plants in rectangular arrays, she would have three [*five*] choices. Each row would have to have the same number of plants. Thus she couldn't do 5 rows with 3 plants and another row with 1 plant. *The number of plants on one side multiplied by the number of plants on the other side has to equal 16. The sides have to be factors of 16.* She could do 4 rows with 4 plants. *This is a square, but squares are also rectangles.* She could do 8 rows with 2 plants or 2 rows with 8 plants. These last two would look different, but they have the same numbers. *There could also be 16 rows with 1 plant or 1 row with 16 plants. The examples show how these are different* [Figure 4-7].

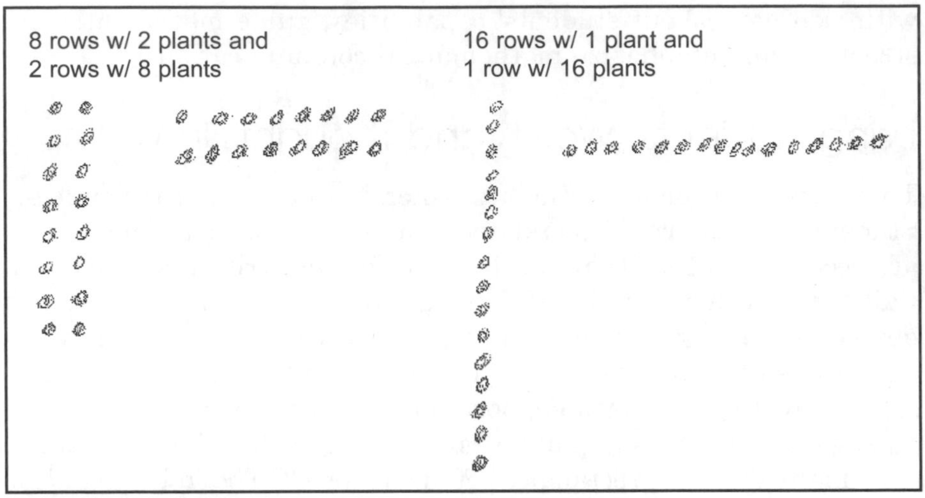

8 rows w/ 2 plants and
2 rows w/ 8 plants

16 rows w/ 1 plant and
1 row w/ 16 plants

Figure 4-7. Garden Illustration

The teacher wasn't comfortable with the students' views of 2 and 8 being different from 8 and 2, and 1 and 16 being different from 16 and 1. She accepted the students' reasoning, however, because she thought they argued successfully that these were different arrangements for the plants. After discussion, she concluded that the students understood that these are the same rectangles, just positioned differently. It provided an opportunity for her to talk about how turning shapes can be used to show they are the same. She used this writing activity as a teaching moment to introduce rotations, one of three important transformations.

Using Complete-the-Statement Exercises

Good mathematical writing requires students to describe their thinking and provide mathematical justification to support their reasoning. These skills require development and become refined and extended over time. One way to help students understand what good mathematical writing involves is to provide them with examples of how to describe their thinking and provide sound mathematical justifications. The following statements illustrate how this process can work with middle school students studying solving two-step equations.

> When solving the equation $5x + 2 = 12$, Joseph subtracts 2 from both sides to get $5x = 10$. He argues, "As long as I do the _____ operation on both sides, the expression is still _____. " [*same, equal*]

> Consider the equation $\frac{1}{2}x - 7 = 13$. The equation can be rewritten without any fractions by _____ each term by _____. The result of this multiplication would give me _____. [*multiplying, 2, x − 14 = 26*]

> In order to show that 12 is the solution to $\frac{1}{4}x - 2 = 1$, I would _____ in place of x. This would give me the expression _____ (provide each step). When the left-hand side is simplified, the equation reads _____. Since this statement is _____, 12 is a solution to the equation. [*substitute 12, $\frac{1}{4}(12) - 2 = 1$, $3 - 2 = 1$ and then $1 = 1$, true*]

The use of such statements helps students to think about how to describe their actions in ways that are mathematically sound. Practice in filling in missing information prepares students to provide details in their mathematical writing that shows their level of mathematical understanding related to the task. Such activities are great tools for promoting mathematical thinking and help students to internalize qualities of good mathematical writing.

Summary

This chapter focused on ways to help students understand what good writing in mathematics looks like and how the teacher can help students to internalize such expectations. The four-element framework was introduced as a way of describing good writing.

Specific strategies for helping students to internalize expectations and standards for good writing include using examples of students' work. The use of such examples to support discussions about improving written responses and recognizing high-quality elements was demonstrated. Other strategies that can help students to understand criteria for good writing were also discussed. In order for students to be successful in writing mathematically, they must understand what is expected of them. Development of these expectations supports mathematics instruction that is rich and emphasizes reasoning and the development of thinking. Emphasis on these cognitive processes is crucial if students are to extend their mathematical understanding through communication.

Chapter 5

Using Writing
With Pairs or Groups

Communication, even written, is not a process that is carried out in isolation. Even if writing is produced for the writer alone, the dialogue becomes a process of clarifying and extending one's own thinking. There is great potential for the initial product to be changed so that the written communication becomes a conversation with oneself; thus thinking and writing are transformed. Teacher-directed lessons may discourage students' clarification of their own ideas, restricting development of conceptual understanding (Kewley, 1998). Variation in instructional presentation has great potential to positively impact the learning of all students. Writing in mathematics can benefit learners when teachers extend their writing tasks to involve pairs or groups of students. In such learning environments, oral communication becomes a major tenet of such practices and will be discussed in depth in the next chapter. Writing can be powerful when pairs or groups engage in the process. This chapter will highlight that process, raise issues related to group selection and structure, discuss what is important instructionally during such exercises, and provide key ideas about the products arising from paired and group work.

Issues of Group Selection and Structure

Selecting membership for pairs or groups can be a difficult task. Teachers strive for a balance between giving students some autonomy in selecting with whom they work and the need to make placements that maximize the potential of learning from collaboration with others. Collaborative experiences provide powerful learning opportunities for all students. These interactive learning opportunities have the prospect of creating vibrant exchanges that support conceptual understanding, giving the benefit of both to all students, whether they are engaged in pairs or in other group configurations, and whether a student is providing or receiving ideas and information. This opportunity for maximized learning is sometimes referred to as the *zone of proximal development.* Blunk (1998) provides a clear summary of the guiding principle for working within the zone of proximal development:

> A student who has the opportunity to work with someone who has a somewhat better understanding of the concept under discussion is more likely to learn than a student who is working with someone of similar ability and understanding of the concept. (p. 207)

Clearly, students benefit from experiences when their own thinking is challenged and can be extended from the contributions of others. The goal of writing in mathematics is to extend the thinking of all students. Various group structures and multiple communicative tasks that focus on mathematical communication have tremendous potential to work with students within a zone of proximal development. Such experiences also provide students with better understanding of the mathematical concepts and the potential to further develop their mathematical literacy. Further discussion of group selection and structures is necessary to provide a comprehensive guide for teachers to consider when forming working peer relationships that benefit all students involved.

Grouping requires careful considerations about students' abilities and instructional goals. Although heterogeneous grouping does have substantive academic benefits for students, there is some evidence supporting other group compositions. Fuchs, Fuchs, Hamlett, and Karns (1998) recommend that high achievers should have ample opportunity to work with other high achievers when working on complex material in order to promote collaborative thinking; however, they also note that high achievers in heterogeneous groups are valuable when the task is less complex. (On complex tasks there is some evidence that heterogeneous grouping may be less effective because the lower achieving students may not have the background necessary to function successfully, whereas the higher achieving students benefit from the deeper thinking of similar-ability students.) The high achievers are provided with an opportunity to construct, and low achievers benefit from the well-reasoned thinking and explanations. In general, research supports the premise that students of all ability levels can be successful in heterogeneous situations (Linchevski & Kutscher, 1998). These studies imply that whereas heterogeneous grouping benefits all students, high achievers may need opportunities to work with other high-ability students during complex tasks. Teachers should consider varying group membership to accommodate these multiple perspectives.

Working in Pairs

What do these guidelines suggest for work in pairs? There may be some consideration for placing students together who have different levels of ability; however, since the communication is basically two-way, some consideration should be given to placing students with a similar level of abilities together. A middle school teacher shared her approach to this dilemma in stating that she divided the class roster into four groups based on ability and then within those groups created pairs by assigning a student from the top of the division with one from the bottom of the division. She reported that this worked well and that students were still able to extend the thinking of their partners while not becoming frustrated by situations in which there was little mathematical substance in the interactions on which to build.

Another teacher reported that he allowed students to self-select a partner for tasks that called for pairs. He found that this worked well most of the time and that students generally selected partners with whom their abilities were similar enough to benefit from the shared experience. He also added that paired arrangements required a high level of comfort between the two students in order for them to work together and communicate effectively. He found that self-selection was more likely to result in pairs with such dynamics.

Working in dyads or pairs provides students with opportunities to reason and argue about important mathematical topics. Work with partners over a period of time has been shown to significantly enhance the quality of reasoning about a topic (Kuhn, Shaw, & Felton, 1997). As students discuss the mathematics topic, they must arrive at a common understanding of the content. Writing extends their thinking as they discuss and agree upon the necessary justification for their responses. Writing extends the benefits of didactic interaction by providing an additional tool for students to use to reflect on their thinking, consolidate their reasoning, and effectively create mathematical arguments. Although students engaged in oral communication are actively involved in sharing strategies and mathematical ideas, there is an added level of processing involved as students work on a task or problem and formulate a written description of their mathematical thinking.

Working in Groups

Research on cooperative learning, which includes pairs of students working together, shows positive effects on achievement in various subjects at various grade levels (Johnson & Johnson, 2000). Various cooperative learning configurations were more effective when compared with competitive learning.

As students relate information, they are engaged in restructuring and elaborating on the material. The writing-process model employed in such situations uses peer responses in ways that help students learn to evaluate one another's writing. Written products from group processing provide growth opportunities for all members to develop their abilities to provide descriptive explanations of mathematical thinking. There is substantive evidence that suggests the best configuration for groups is based on mixed academic ability. A common practice is to configure groups of four with one high-ability, two medium-ability, and one low-ability student. Although teachers may at times select groups based on similarity of academic ability, such arrangements should be used infrequently, and perhaps then only in situations involving complex tasks (Fuchs et al., 1998). Experimental studies show equal benefits for high, average, and low achievers when compared to the performance of academic-level counterparts in control groups (Slavin, 1996). In fact, the very highest achievers, those in the top 10% at pretest, showed particularly large positive effects from cooperative learning when separated in the analysis. Students who engage in providing explanations as part of the group processing benefit regardless of their academic-ability level.

Group size should be kept manageable; three to four appears to have the greatest success in promoting student learning. Groups that are larger than four or five students do not promote the participation of all members, which is vital for realizing the academic benefits of group tasks. Large groups may give students an opportunity to hide and not contribute to the task at hand (Fiechtner & Davis,

1992; Slavin, 1995). There is also more positive building of interdependence in smaller size groups; larger groups experience greater difficulty developing a sense of cohesion. Teachers who are somewhat new at various grouping structures report that beginning with dyads provides positive experiences for getting students prepared for working in larger groups. Teachers also indicate that initially they select tasks that are shorter and less complex so that confidence is built and students have an opportunity to get used to working with peers. The complexity of the tasks then becomes more elaborate, which builds nicely into increasing the size of the group so that more individuals bring their thinking into the learning situation.

Implementing Collaborative Writing-to-Learn Experiences

A central goal of collaborative experiences is to develop students' abilities to reason mathematically. Research involving peer-to-peer interactions in mathematics (O'Connor, 1998) confirms that poor performance is highly correlated with nonresponsive feedback, which is characterized by being told the correct answer by peers with no further elaboration or description, whereas high achievement is related to behaviors characterized by elaborate descriptions and explanations to others (Webb, 1991). Writing provides a natural tool that focuses on extending students' abilities to provide rich and sound mathematical descriptions and explanations. As students work in pairs or groups, teachers can use writing as a way of focusing interactions on the development of mathematical reasoning. Such mathematical reasoning is captured and generated through students' work in explaining and describing their thinking. As students record their thoughts and ideas, they are required to reflect on the adequacy of their ideas, both in terms of their mathematical correctness and the qualities of the communication.

In any collaborative experience, students must be willing to take risks. Revealing one's thinking can be threatening for students, whether the information is written or oral. Writing in pairs or groups provides a setting in which students create a common product. Students must share their thinking about a task and formulate shared ideas to create a written product. In order for students to agree on the content of the writing, there must be discussion and a sharing of ideas, leading to an agreement of what constitutes a sound response to the task. Such learning experiences further emphasize the importance of students' understanding of what constitutes good mathematical communication, as defined in the previous chapter.

What are some guidelines that mathematics teachers should keep in mind as they implement pair and group writing tasks? Following are some common principles that guide the positive implementation of learning situations that progress beyond individually oriented learning:

- Select tasks that are challenging enough to engage the students but not so complex as to generate irresolvable frustration.

- All members of the group must participate. Assign roles for group members and insist that all members of the group share their ideas and thinking.

- Monitor groups and clarify tasks, but develop the expectation that students must rely on the input of their group before asking for assistance.

- Emphasize the collaborative nature of working in real-world settings.

- Set clear time limits.

- Develop group behavior expectations.

Task Selection

Chapter 2 listed five components that provide a useful approach to selecting tasks that promote rich mathematical understanding. These components (Kilpatrick, Swafford, & Findell, 2001)—conceptual understanding, procedural fluency, strategic competence, adaptive reasoning, and productive dispositions—can provide a means for reviewing the mathematics in selected tasks. It is important to vary the emphasis of communicative tasks so that students develop a broad understanding of multiple mathematical topics, competencies, skills, and reasoning approaches.

When providing group or pair writing exercises, teachers should consider two key characteristics that will make the task appropriate for collaborative learning. First, the task should be open-ended enough so that it requires several sentences or short paragraphs to respond to the prompt or problem. Chapter 2 provides information on how to modify typical problems and exercises so that they provide rich communication opportunities. Second, the task should encourage communication and discussion. Some tasks may lack the complexity to engage students beyond a few minutes. Tasks that cover multiple concepts or ideas are best for group and pair writing exercises. Multistep problems often provide a rich context in which students can discuss strategies, approaches, and mathematical justifications. Encouraging students to find alternative approaches and solutions and requiring students to answer *why* support collaboration and communication of mathematical ideas. Tasks should encourage reflection on the mathematics that students already know, extend to ideas and concepts that they need to figure out, and promote the selection of appropriate mathematical concepts or strategies.

Member Participation

It is imperative that every member participate in the task. This can be as simple as a student repeating or clarifying what others in the group are saying, but each member should participate in order to extend his or her understanding. One way to promote involvement is to have the students develop some ideas or approaches individually before they share their information with their peers. This will give each student an opportunity to contribute. It also gives the teacher some time to provide assistance to those students who are likely to struggle with the task. Teachers might consider assigning roles to various members of a group, particularly when observations reveal that a member of a group might not be actively engaged in the group processing. Such roles might include reading the information, recording ideas in draft form, writing the ideas in final form, checking or editing the work, or presenting the findings to the teacher or class. Throughout the year, these roles can be rotated to various members of the group.

Group Monitoring and Interdependence

Teachers should visit each group initially and regularly to clarify the task and monitor individual student involvement. Students, especially when they initially begin working together, often solicit information from the teacher. Clarifying the nature of the task and providing guidance is extremely important; however, members of groups must also learn to be interdependent on the expertise from the collective experiences and knowledge of the group members. A good rule to promote is that a question will be answered only if it has first been raised to the entire group and the members of the group have had an opportunity to respond. Responding by raising questions or providing a scaffold for the necessary information will force the group to collaborate to respond to the teacher's question or information. Remember that students learn more when they respond and discuss ideas and concepts with their group members. The goal is for students to prepare a common outcome and share the tasks and responsibilities for the task and the written product. Producing a written product requires the students to synthesize their ideas, develop compelling arguments and justifications, and communicate those ideas effectively.

Real-World Collaboration

An important skill that students develop from collaborative experiences such as these is the ability to make decisions based on careful reflection. Working on a common goal and developing approaches to address the task are vital workplace skills. Collaborative learning experiences provide students with opportunities to develop team skills that require working together to be successful. This gives students a feel for real-world settings that require the application of refined social skills, higher level thinking approaches, and clear and concise communication skills.

Communication skills; adaptability and creative thinking; group effectiveness, interpersonal skills, negotiation and teamwork; and organizational effectiveness and leadership are the skills listed in U.S. Department of Labor publications for tomorrow's workforce (Carnevale, Gainer, & Meltzer, 1988). Students should develop an appreciation for the multifaceted nature of the group or paired writing tasks and see how their participation fosters the development of thinking and social skills that are valued in the real-world environment, particularly in work and community affairs.

Time Limits

Time is extremely important to teachers. The curriculum requires the efficient and effective use of time. In addition to selecting tasks that are rich and powerful as discussed throughout this book, clear time limits should be established for collaborative learning exercises. What teachers must also consider is the trade-off between time and student engagement. Students working on tasks in pairs or groups will be much more engaged in learning than students in individual work or teacher-directed instruction. Clarifying the task, developing clear guidelines and rules so that students get into their collaborative configurations and begin work immediately, and setting some time limitations will make collaborative learning experiences more effective. Teachers will need to monitor the amount of time that various activities take in order to become better able to predict an acceptable amount of time to allow for these writing tasks. Teachers will also want to work with groups to make sure they are paying attention to each other and are working efficiently. Getting students to be committed to making the groups work effectively is important in making sure that time spent in pair or group activities promotes learning. Initially, the teacher should set time limits and negotiate with students if more time is needed. When students realize that they have a certain amount of time in which to complete a task, they are likely to stay focused and earnestly try to work within the time constraints. Teachers may consider having a timekeeper in each group to monitor the progress of the group and remind members of the time remaining to complete the task.

Group Behavior Expectations

A basic consideration is to keep the rules for collaborative work simple and few. These include the acceptable level of noise during talking, taking turns and allowing every group member to participate, and procedures and expectations for the written product. Teachers might have discussions with students about the rules. Allowing students to participate in developing common expectations makes it more likely that each student will understand the rules and their importance. It is also good practice to have demonstrations or role-plays from a group on how they should conduct themselves while working on a common task. Teachers can also model good group processing and communication skills. When groups are performing well, it is important to let the group members know that their conduct and actions are examples of good group or pair collaboration. In addition, if students understand what the written product requires, including any format or specific guidelines the teacher would like to establish, there is less confusion about what to do, which saves time, reduces the amount of talking, and results in more goal-oriented behaviors. Groups or pairs should be engaged in ways that make their work effective and efficient. Nagel (2001, p. 170) provides five rules to guide group discussions. These five guidelines, which summarize some key expectations to communicate to students about their group behaviors, follows.

- Be concise. (Stick to the topic.)
- Listen. (Pay attention.)

- Reflect. (Repeat something from a previous person's comments and, I would add, provide your ideas and thoughts grounded in mathematical reasoning.)
- Contribute. (Everyone is included.)
- Respect others. (Avoid blame, maintain confidentiality.)

Examples of Collaborative Writing

The following examples were produced by a group of three students in an introductory algebra class in a middle school. This work is especially significant because this particular class was composed of students who did not perform well in their pre-algebra class. The writing produced by this group indicates the power of reflective thinking that is promoted when students work collaboratively and write about their mathematical reasoning.

In Figure 5-1, students were asked to discuss in their groups how they would solve $18x^3 + 48x^2 = 32x$ and then write a description of their approach.

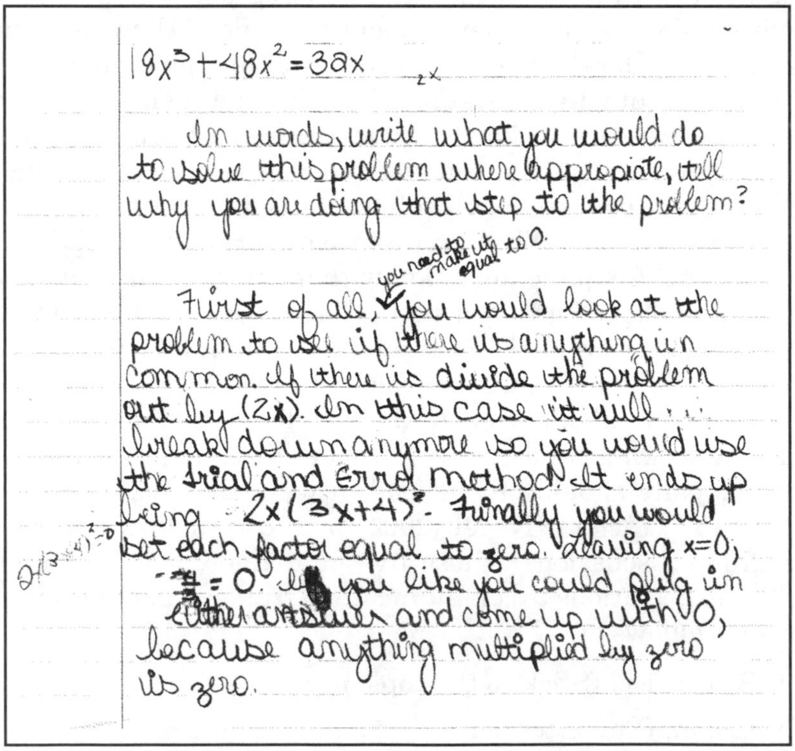
$18x^3+48x^2=32x$

In words, write what you would do to solve this problem where appropiate, tell why you are doing that step to the problem?

you need to make it equal to 0.

First of all, you would look at the problem to see if there is anything in common. If there is divide the problem out by (2x). In this case it will ... break down anymore so you would use the trial and Error method. It ends up being $2x(3x+4)^2$. Finally you would set each factor equal to zero. Leaving x=0, $-\frac{4}{3}=0$. If you like you could plug in either answer and come up with 0, because anything multiplied by zero is zero.

$2(3x+4)^2=0$

Figure 5-1. Collaborative Product for Equation Task

The students' writing is remarkably concise and represents a solid understanding of the process necessary to solve an equation requiring multiple steps. There are two important observations to make about the students' writing: an insertion of additional information in line one and a word that is erased in line four. The insertion illustrates that the collaborative process provided an opportunity to refine the group's method. The added information demonstrates that students were discussing important mathematical concepts connected to the procedures they would employ. The insertion, "you need to make it equal to 0," is an important piece of information that is revisited later in the writing. On line four, the word *not* is erased, showing that the students redirected their assessment of their approach. The change demonstrates that students were able to use the writing process to reflect on their work and make significant modifications in their procedures as well as the underlying mathematical reasons. An additional note written by the students in the margin, $2x (3x + 4)^2 = 0$, also shows that the students were thinking about the importance of continuing to write their expression as an equation. This is an important step because it helps to illustrate that one or both of these factors must be zero—an illustration of the zero product property. The teacher had continually emphasized this property as a basis for setting each factor equal to zero to solve the equation.

The group's written product reveals how the students were able to think about the problem. Writing their thoughts provides some permanence to their ideas and becomes a vehicle for reflecting and refining their thinking. The students show that they have a clear understanding of the procedures necessary to solve the equation using factoring. They illustrate that it is important to get all the terms on one side of the equal sign, check for common factors, and further factor the resulting expression, if possible. They then show that setting each factor equal to zero will yield a solution to the equation. Although some additional thoughts demonstrating that they had verified their solution would have been desirable, these students provided a clear and accurate description of their approach to finding a solution to the equation. The written product is especially significant, given that students with histories of lower academic performance are frequently reluctant writers, particularly when it comes to writing about mathematics processes and concepts.

For the next problem, pairs of students were asked to complete the task shown in Figure 5-2:

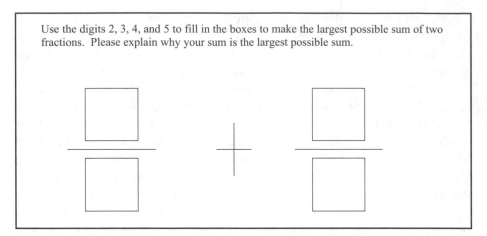

Use the digits 2, 3, 4, and 5 to fill in the boxes to make the largest possible sum of two fractions. Please explain why your sum is the largest possible sum.

Figure 5-2. Writing Task for Student Pairs

Let's consider how two different pairs responded to the task. The fifth-grade teacher had formed the pairs of students by identifying the students who had the greatest difficulty understanding fraction concepts and pairing them with either a high-ability or average-ability student who had mastered the concept. The teacher was also careful to place the struggling students with a partner who would be supportive and encourage full participation. Both of the responses discussed here are products from such student pairs.

Both pairs were able to successfully solve the problem obtaining a sum of $3\,5/6$. The first response (Figure 5-3) shows a systematic approach to finding the answer. The students realized that the smallest

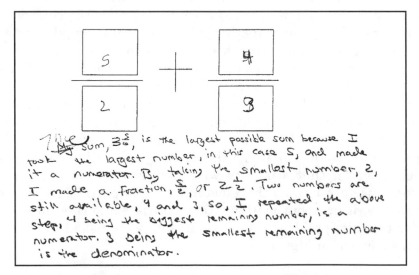

Figure 5-3. Response From First Pair on Fraction Task

digit should be in the denominator of the fraction. The response shows some insight in placing the largest digit with the smallest digit to make the fraction $5/2$ and then repeating the process with the remaining two digits. Unfortunately, the response does not elaborate on the reasoning behind their actions. Why does placing the largest digit as the numerator and the smallest as the denominator produce the largest possible fraction?

The second response (Figure 5-4) is somewhat better in providing some logic. The students wrote that the reason their fractions had the largest possible sum was "because the numorators [sic] are the larger of the four #'s." They continue, "The numeroators [sic] are bigger than the demonator [sic] so the answer while [sic] be larger." These students were better able to communicate some reasoning behind their placement of the numbers; however, the response still lacks key ideas about the role of the numerator and denominator in determining the size of the fraction.

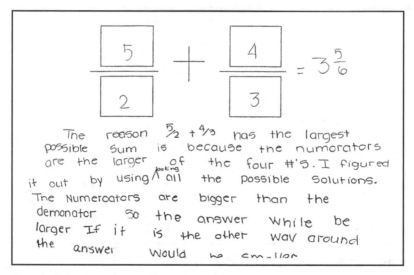

Figure 5-4. Response From Second Pair on Fraction Task

This task provided a rich opportunity for two students to work together on a task that was challenging, requiring both to provide input that would lead to the correct answer. The prompt required students to provide some justification for their response. Although the responses contain numerous spelling and mechanical errors, the teacher was pleased that the majority of the pairs recognized a relationship between the size of the denominators and the size of the fraction. As students worked in pairs, they were able to provide input about why they would place the numbers in a specific way. The discussions of multiple approaches forced students to justify why their answer was correct. The student pairs had to reach a consensus that they had the largest possible sum and had to be able to tell why they were confident of their response. Writing and group processing reinforced addition of fractions as an operation while building essential conceptual understanding of the relationship between numerators and denominators in determining the size of a fraction.

Some pairs of students listed every possible combination and determined the sums. The teacher recognized the validity of this approach and was pleased that students were able to determine all the possible combinations, find the sums of the various pairs of fractions, and order the sums to determine their answer to the task. In the class processing of the task, the teacher began with students sharing this approach to the problem. The students' response pictured in Figure 5-5 typifies this approach. The teacher complimented the students on their thoroughness in responding to the task.

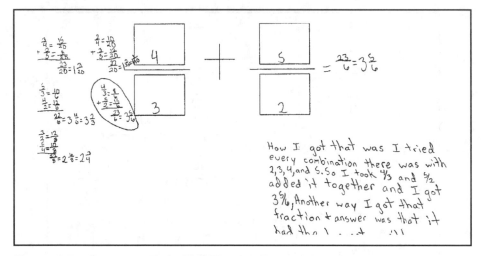

Figure 5-5. Response From Third Pair on Fraction Task

She then asked if anyone had an approach that didn't require finding the sums of all the combinations. The pair who produced the response in Figure 5-4 shared their approach. The discussion that followed emphasized that both approaches were correct but that the second was more efficient because it drew on important mathematical concepts and relationships and did not rely on computation. The teacher asked students how they could have improved their written responses. Two factors to improve the written explanations were identified by the students: Do a better job describing why, and pay closer attention to spelling *numerator* and *denominator* correctly.

Summary

An effective way to engage mathematics students in writing is to provide opportunities to work in pairs and groups. This requires students to reflect on and process important mathematical ideas and concepts and then reach a consensus on how to best communicate that information. In addition to supporting students' growth toward mathematical literacy, group and pair work develops important social and critical thinking skills. Written work as the product of group and pair processing adds a reflective element, which requires students to carefully consider the mathematics being used.

Forming pairs and groups can be a difficult process. Although homogeneous groups might be used in some instances, such as when working on tasks that are very complex, research supports forming groups that are heterogeneous in ability. Such configurations support both high-ability and low-ability students in extending their mathematical understanding. The important factor related to performance appears to be whether the students are engaged in explaining and reasoning during the process. Students who interact and explain more make better academic gains. Writing provides an element that can further support the process of explaining and reasoning while also promoting the engagement of all the students.

Groups and pairs have to function well in order for the students to realize the potential learning benefits. Some factors to consider include selecting tasks that are challenging enough to engage the students but not so complex as to generate irresolvable frustration, making sure that all members of the group are participating and sharing their ideas, monitoring groups and clarifying tasks while requiring groups to discuss questions and issues before seeking the teacher's assistance, emphasizing the real-world nature of collaborative work, setting clear time limits, and developing expectations for group behavior. It requires careful attention and effort to establish effective group work, but the benefits in terms of building students' mathematical understanding and the ability to communicate mathematically are significant.

Chapter 6

Connecting Written and Oral Communication

Throughout this work, writing has been emphasized as a language tool that serves in forming meaning and building mathematical understanding. A case was presented in chapter 3 that writing should not be perceived as an add-on to the mathematics curriculum. Students as well as teachers should view writing as a vital learning tool that helps students to develop a deep understanding of concepts, ideas, procedures, and processes while providing the teacher with a tremendous means of developing students' mathematical literacy. The case was also made that the effective implementation of writing in mathematics necessitates consideration of the relationship between written and oral communication. The reader was made more familiar with this link in Chapter 5, in which peer and group tasks were discussed as one way of implementing writing in the mathematics classroom. This chapter builds on these earlier discussions by elaborating how classroom experiences can connect written and oral communication. A model based on classroom practice is presented to help teachers understand this relationship and build classroom communities that use language to enhance students' mathematical understanding.

The Writing and Speaking Mathematics Relationship

What is the relationship between writing and speaking mathematics? Although spoken and written communication, in general, have different purposes (Meaney, 2002), the emphasis on mathematical communication is to develop students' understanding of mathematics while also improving their communicative abilities. Meaney argues that mathematics involves many complex ideas and that writing as an integral part of the activity will involve a steady checking and reflecting on what is being discussed and done. He also argues that students can use writing to support reflection, and he cautions that students should not see reflection as secondary to the written task. Students who experience difficulty with language will require scaffolding and modeling of the effective use of language as a tool for reflection. These ideas are consistent with a seamless view of writing in mathematics, further emphasizing the importance of spoken language as part of the mathematics learning trajectory.

Experiences that provide oral and written communication opportunities for students are more likely to promote an exchange and elaborated discussion so that a conceptual level of mathematical understanding is developed. Communication is a tool for critical thinking as students use both written and oral forms to analyze, evaluate, and synthesize important mathematical concepts, ideas, and problems (see chapter 3 of Nagel, 2001). This view of vibrant mathematics communities, in which students are engaged in oral and written communication, differs from traditional approaches to mathematics, in which teachers do most of the explaining and demonstrating. In this type of instruction student talk plays a central role in developing a deeper mathematical understanding.

How do teachers promote this communication-rich environment? First, the community is dependent on connections between writing and speaking. The reflective and generative nature of writing to promote a deeper understanding of ideas and concepts should not be underestimated. When both forms of communication are treated as fundamental to mathematics teaching and learning, students will benefit. In order to better understand this relationship, let's consider the characteristics of such a community. The following description draws from Hufferd-Ackles, Fuson, and Sherin (2004). Their perspectives are extended in arguing that the same framework for a math-talk learning community is enriched by including explicit and well-planned components that require students to use written communication to build mathematical knowledge and understanding. In fact, research on problem solving shows that students who write descriptions of their problem-solving processes are significantly more successful than students who think aloud while solving the problems (Pugalee, 2004). There is tremendous untapped potential in implementing instruction that draws on the benefits of both written and oral communication in mathematics.

The Nature of Speaking-Writing Mathematics

The research on communication in mathematics classrooms presented by Hufferd-Ackles, Fuson, and Sherin (2004) gives a solid foundation for considering the nature of communication in mathematics learning. The framework includes four components, or developmental trajectories: questioning, explaining mathematical thinking, sources of mathematical ideas, and responsibility for learning. I would argue that written communication extends the capabilities of students to think about their own mathematical understanding as well as to consider and evaluate the thinking of others. This speaking-writing mathematics link is a powerful vehicle for promoting students' mathematical learning. Table 6-1 is an adaptation of this work and focuses on student characteristics at the highest level of this framework.

Table 6-1. Characteristics of Highest Level for Speaking-Writing Mathematics

Questioning	Explaining Mathematical Thinking	Source of Ideas	Responsibility for Learning
Students initiate questions, focus on *why,* requiring reflection and resulting in justification and mathematical reasoning.	Students provide rich descriptions of their mathematical actions and thoughts. Precision develops as students use mathematical language.	Students share ideas and thinking, thus stimulating classroom discourse. Students work together to compare and contrast mathematical ideas and approaches.	Feedback builds confidence and helps students to develop standards for mathematical thinking. Students question and analyze their own thinking and that of others.

Adapted from Hufferd-Ackles, Fuson, & Sherin (2004)

Let's consider the mathematical power evidenced in this level of student engagement. Bear in mind that these are the characteristics at the most advanced level of the model. First, students' questions focus on *why,* necessitating a careful deliberation and reflection on important mathematical concepts and ideas. Justification and reasoning are hallmarks of this type of interaction. It is this level of thinking that supports a more sophisticated mathematical understanding and helps students to construct complex chains of mathematical reasoning. This type of thinking and reasoning is essential in students' developing and evaluating mathematical arguments and proofs (NCTM, 2000), an important habit of mind built on reasoning and justification.

Second, students provide richer descriptions of their strategies, including mathematically sound justifications. The NCTM (2000) standards envision mathematical communication as maturing, so that students demonstrate increasingly different ways of justifying their procedures and results with greater precision in the use of mathematical language, argumentation, and explanation. Students consistently provide thorough descriptions of their thinking and realize that their choices and actions must be grounded in sound mathematics. Students organize their thinking, reflect on the mathematics, and produce coherent descriptions of those processes.

Third, students are confident in their mathematical thinking and communication and are capable of shaping and expanding the mathematics being learned. As students' skills in mathematical communication become more refined and their reasoning skills more developed, they will provide ideas and information that can stimulate classroom discussion. Students' strategies and approaches provide robust opportunities for teachers to build on this thinking to achieve the goals of the lesson. The teacher assists students in forming a productive mathematical community while providing some quality control for the outcomes (McNair, 1998). The NCTM (2000) standards affirm that communication can promote students' learning of new ideas and concepts as they engage in acting out situations, giving verbal accounts and explanations, drawing and using diagrams, and writing and using mathematical symbols. In this environment, students explore what they know and understand about mathematics, raise questions about what is unclear, and apply reasoning and judgment in constructing mathematical knowledge.

Fourth, students' communication provides opportunities for clarifying and understanding mathematics. As students question and analyze the thinking of others, they are promoting a solid mathematical understanding not only for their peers but also for themselves. Communication involves listening, restating, paraphrasing, questioning, comparing and contrasting, interpreting, and analyzing one's own ideas and those of others. Students can learn from the mathematical insights of others. As stated in the standards (NCTM, 2000), students who listen and question the claims of others also learn to become critical thinkers of mathematics.

A Model of Speaking-Writing Mathematics

The model offered in Figure 6-1 depicts the power of oral and written communication in mathematics, demonstrating their interactive and interdependent nature while recognizing the influence of communication on classroom discourse. An important component of the model is the feedback loop that occurs through various classroom settings: the students working together in pairs or groups, the teacher's facilitation of the lesson, and the discourse involving the

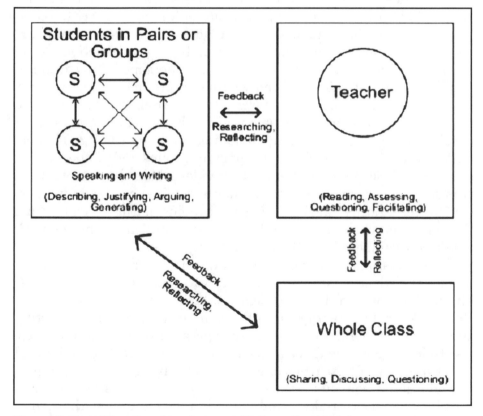

Figure 6-1.   Writing-Speaking to Learn Mathematics Model

whole class. This feedback loop promotes reflection on the mathematics being considered. This reflection occurs when students are challenged to consider their ideas and thoughts and evaluate the clarity and accurateness of their mathematical thinking, which is revealed in their oral communication and further refined and polished in the written products; thus, the feedback loop stimulates reflecting and revising as students build mathematical understanding. The two-directional arrows depict how ideas influence communication between the involved participants shaping the content and purpose of what is shared.

The model shows how students, working in pairs or groups, are involved in a mutual sharing of ideas that influence how mathematical concepts are developed and learned. This interactive environment is characterized by the involvement of all the students as they speak and write to learn mathematics. This communication involves levels of critical thinking as students engage in describing, justifying, arguing, and generating mathematical ideas and solutions. As students interact with the teacher during their pair or group processing, they are guided to consider and evaluate the mathematics relevant to the task. The teacher considers the oral and written communication of the students and provides structure and support through questioning and sometimes small-group instruction.

As shown in the model, the teacher has a phenomenal role in shaping the nature of this speaking-writing environment. The teacher carefully considers the oral and written ideas from the students. The teacher facilitates the development of mathematical understanding through reading, assessing, questioning, and facilitating. This occurs as the teacher interacts with pairs or groups and as the teacher channels whole-class discussion or provides whole-class instruction. It is the teacher who "promotes students' confidence, flexibility, perseverance, curiosity, and inventiveness in doing mathematics through the use of appropriate tasks and by engaging students in mathematical discourse" (NCTM, 1991, p. 104).

Whole-class participation is important in this process. Opportunities for the whole class to process what was learned are essential for effective instruction. The whole class shares, questions, and assesses the thinking that emerges from the pairs or groups. This reporting time allows students to consider other perspectives and approaches. As students reflect on these ideas, their own ideas will be challenged and supported. The teacher might consider giving pairs or groups a few additional moments to revise their written products. Other teachers choose to have students individually respond to how their written work was supported or would be changed as a result of the class discussion. Although either approach is valuable, giving students an opportunity to revise their written responses to the task provides a stronger support for the writing process and extends the collaborative process for developing mathematical understanding.

Examples of Speaking-Writing to Learn Mathematics

The example in Figure 6-2 demonstrates how speaking and writing can provide a powerful tool for learning mathematics. The example comes from an eighth-grade classroom in which students were learning about similar triangle relationships. The classroom teacher had worked to develop some classroom expectations about writing and working together. Students frequently responded to the writing of others, providing information about the strengths and weaknesses of the writing. To evaluate students' written responses, students

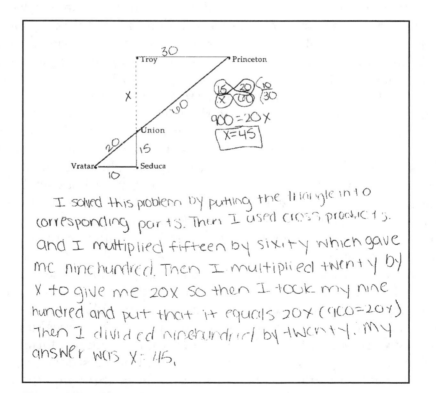

Figure 6-2.   Similar Triangle Problem

applied a rubric that was a simplified version of the one used for the state-mandated writing test given at that grade level. Rubrics and assessment will be discussed in greater detail in part III of this book. In this example, students worked individually to solve the task and write an explanation of their methods and conclusions. Pairs then exchanged papers and assessed the quality (both mathematical content and writing) of the papers.

This student's work shows evidence of understanding the concept of similar triangles and an excellent understanding of the procedure for using proportions in solving for the missing distance. Although the answer to the problem is correct, there were some problems identified by the student's partner when they exchanged papers. The paper did receive a top score using the rubric, but the following question was raised: "Good job with setting up the problem and solving the fractions. How do you know you have corresponding parts? 45 what? Inches?" The idea of corresponding parts was important as the basis for solving the problem. The student never stated that she concluded that the triangles were similar. Without this conclusion, even though the student's actions demonstrate that she was working under this assumption, the description of her thinking has a major gap. The explanation shows a pairing of the various corresponding parts of the triangle. The student's explanation describes what she did with these numbers: multiplying 15 by 60 and 20 by x to get $900 = 20x$, then dividing by 20 to get the answer of x = 45.

Once the students had assessed the papers of their peers, the papers were returned and a whole-class discussion followed. The teacher was pleased with how the students used similar triangle relationships to solve the problem. She was very specific, however, in stressing that many students used that relationship without explicitly stating it. She emphasized that there needed to be some determination that the triangles were similar. The teacher said that the mathematical model for the problem was based on similar triangles, but that the mathematical relationships to definitively state that conclusion were not present. Through leading questions, the teacher asked students how they could make a case for the similarity of the triangles. Students directed their attention to the angles. They quickly offered that the angles with a vertex at Union were vertical angles, so they were equal. Several then added that the angles formed at Seduca and Troy were right angles. Several other students questioned how they could know this with confidence. Students then realized that their model of similar triangles was based on the best model they could construct for the situation. If the angles formed at Seduca and Troy were right angles, then the two remaining angles would have to be congruent; thus, the triangles would be similar. This was a powerful discussion of how real-world applications depend on making observations about relationships. The teacher shared the goals she had for the problem: Students would work with relationships involving similarity and would grapple with a real-world application that required them to make some assumptions about their mathematical model. The teacher also asked students how they would write their final answers, based on the discussion. One student offered that the answers were approximations based on applying a model of similar triangles, so the answer would be approximately 45 miles.

Students' working individually, evaluating their thinking through peer assessment, and using the written products with the feedback questions as a way of promoting a whole-class discussion shows how the speaking-writing communication model provides exciting and engaging opportunities for students to study mathematics. The example illustrates how each piece—student work, peer interaction, and the whole-class discussion—helped the teacher to meet the goals of the lesson. In this particular instance, the teacher did not have the students revisit their written explanations. This may have been a missed opportunity that would have provided students with time to reflect and internalize the important discussion about evidence for similarity and the appropriateness of their mathematical models.

Students worked in small groups as they solved the following problem: "Yan has 3 green chips, 4 blue chips, and 1 red chip. What part of the chips are green, blue, and red?" The teacher had worked for about 5 months on developing writing skills routinely as part of this third-grade math class. The students were asked to tell how their group did the problem. In Figure 6-3, students used different colors (green, blue, and red) to fill in ovals to represent the chips. The number of chips was also written in the corresponding color.

The computation at the top of the figure shows that the students knew they needed to determine the total number of chips so they could represent the parts. The students' language reinforces how important they considered this information. "We added . . . together for finding what part the whole was. It was 8." Students also described the relationship in fractions. "Fractions have a whole on the bottom and a part on the top." Their step 4 relates that they formed three fractions to represent the different colors. Finally, they checked to see if any of the fractions could be smaller: "and the blue can." The reduced fraction and the process the students used to reduce $4/8$ to $1/2$ can be found on the side of the written response.

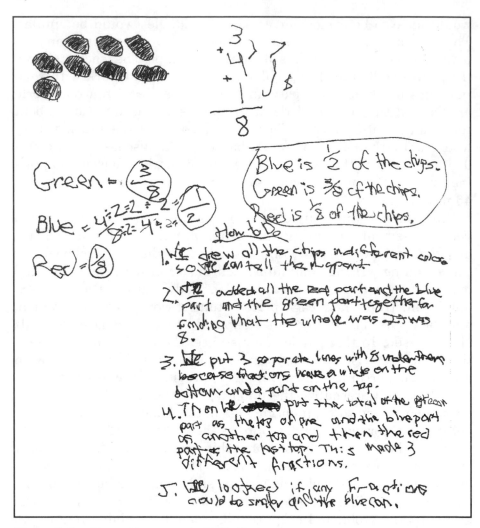

Figure 6-3. Group Response to Ratio Task

This is a strong piece of writing for a group of third graders. They demonstrated a clear approach for finding the answer to the task and were able to articulate their thinking. The power of multiple voices is evident in their response. The systematic process reflected in the writing is the product of oral discussion, problem solving, and reflecting on the process. Writing provided students with a goal that required further organization of their thinking as well as justification for their decisions. Key mathematical concepts related to understanding ratios and comparisons are evident in this response. The teacher has an important artifact that provides a window into what students understood about part and whole relationships and how to use those relationships to talk about real objects.

Alternative Writing Opportunities

Teachers should consider other formats that promote student communication and engage them in constructing and generating mathematical ideas and concepts, thus supporting mathematical literacy. Teachers often find that conceptual tools can be implemented to assist students as they reflect and consolidate their thinking about important mathematics. Such conceptual tools can be especially productive if the written task involves processing text. A popular tool among teachers is a reading strategy that helps students to organize key mathematical ideas. Speaking and writing are central to the task while giving structure to the final product. The following example (Figure 6-4) from a fourth-grade lesson on pyramids demonstrates the promise of such techniques in helping students to comprehend important mathematical concepts.

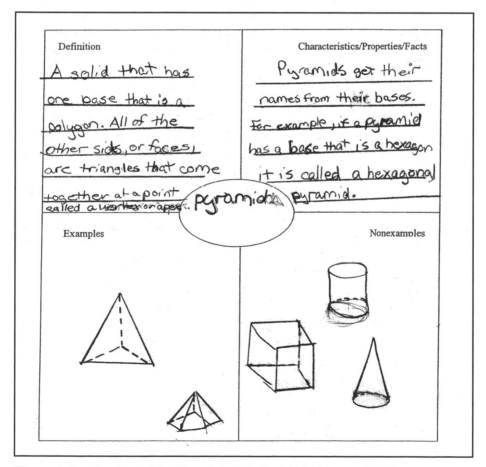

Figure 6-4.   One Model for Organizing Students' Thinking and Writing

This model requires students working in either pairs or groups to provide four key elements that emphasize understanding of pyramids: a definition; key characteristics, properties, or facts; examples; and nonexamples. Teachers can modify this strategy to accommodate different learning targets. Notice that students provide complete thoughts instead of lists of ideas. The teacher developed clear expectations (see chapter 4) about acceptable responses for this type of product. The students' work in this example is a positive illustration of the four elements of good mathematical writing: it is done with a purpose that is evident in the written product; the structure and development provide details, arguments, justifications, and assertions that lead to a conclusion; information and ideas are conveyed in a precise and concise manner; and basic grammar and mechanics are evident. These students demonstrate a clear understanding of pyramids and have a broad conceptual base that is evident through considering characteristics and properties as well as examples and nonexamples. Writing provides a tool for students to process text, reflect on key mathematical concepts, and consolidate their thinking through a concise and instrumental written record of those ideas.

The pyramid example also incorporates two key features for building conceptual understanding: examples and nonexamples. These are considered essential in helping students to understand attributes and properties (Clements, 2000; Park, 1984; Tennyson & Park, 1980). The responses for this category do not have to be diagrams or drawings. For example, work on the concept of whole numbers might include 0, 1, 2, and so on. Teachers might communicate that examples and nonexamples must account for certain possibilities. In the whole-number example, it is important for students to include zero because this number distinguishes the set of numbers from a set containing natural numbers. Nonexamples might include fractions, decimals, and negative numbers.

Summary

This chapter provided a model for thinking about emphasizing speaking and writing to help students learn mathematics. The chapter builds on earlier chapters focusing on the writing process. A framework for considering classroom talk as a central component of mathematical learning was presented. Four key elements of that framework provide a way of thinking about speaking and writing as communication tools that promote mathematical literacy (Hufferd-Ackles, Fuson, & Sherin, 2004). First, students ask questions that focus on *why,* thus requiring careful reflection on important mathematics. Second, richer student descriptions provide information on strategies and mathematical justification for those strategies. Third, students become confident in their mathematical thinking as they extend their ability to communicate mathematical ideas. Fourth, opportunities for clarifying and understanding mathematics promote students' understanding and learning.

A model and examples that underscore how speaking and writing help students to learn important mathematics was provided. The model includes students working together and discussing important ideas in pair or group settings. This interaction, mediated by the teacher's facilitation, provides a feedback loop through which students reflect and assess their mathematical understanding and communication. Whole-class discussion, as indicated in the model, provides additional occasions for the pairs or groups and the teacher to bring together the ideas of the class, discuss important concepts and strategies that emerged during the processing of the task, and raise key questions that further stimulate students' reflection and consideration of the mathematics being studied. In addition, whole-class discussion provides an opportunity for students to once again consider the mathematical soundness of their responses and the degree to which their mathematical communication is also effective in concisely and descriptively conveying their thinking (Silver & Stein, 1996). The importance of giving students opportunities to revise written products is emphasized. These learning exercises, mediated by rich verbal and written communication, promote mathematical understanding and engage students in formidable ways so that they have ownership of their learning.

Assessing

Chapter
7

Managing Assessment
of Students' Writing

Assessing students' writing can be an overwhelming task, especially for teachers of mathematics who have little expertise and training in writing instruction. The written products that students create as part of their mathematics learning are valuable sources of information about their depth of mathematical understanding. These written products provide a rich and extensive view of the mathematics that students know and their capabilities in applying that knowledge. Such assessment measures provide substantively more information than traditional measures, which frequently focus on the correctness of a single answer or response. Through writing, students record their thinking. Their products become a window into their cognitive processing while they are engaged in mathematical tasks, yet the assessment of these written products can be daunting. This chapter will discuss some general assessment issues, methods for assessing students' written work, and specific ideas and examples of assessment approaches in practice.

There are two major issues that teachers frequently raise about assessing students' writing. The first deals with time and material management. Student writing generates much more paper than other forms of assessment. There are questions related to how to manage all of this paper. A related question deals with finding time to assess these products. The second major issue deals with what they should be assessing. Teachers want to know what they should be looking for in students' writing. They also want to know how to balance assessing the mathematics and the quality of the writing.

Time and Material Management Issues

Classroom time is valuable. Teachers today are especially pressed to use time efficiently, given the demands of the curriculum. Mathematics teachers are also especially sensitive about using time wisely, given that students' performance in mathematics and literacy is likely to be formally assessed through local, state, and national initiatives or requirements. The first six chapters presented a strong case for why writing in mathematics is important for promoting students' mathematical understanding. The issues of time and materials management do not have to become burdensome by-products of implementing a writing emphasis in mathematics teaching. Part II discussed approaches that help to make writing a seamless part of mathematics instruction. This type of implementation promotes student time on-task and protects valuable classroom instructional time. As teachers and students become more comfortable with these instructional processes, they will become more time-efficient. The initial time investment is worth the payoff in promoting student learning.

What about how to manage all of the extra paper? A key to keeping up with students' papers is to give responsibility to the students. I've seen teachers use various methods for managing this type of student work. One effective practice is to have students keep a journal or notebook in which they complete their writing assignments. Some teachers prefer not to use spiral notebooks, so that they can collect single assignments without having to take the entire notebooks. Either format will work fine, depending on the preference of the individual teacher. Teachers will have to strongly and consistently communicate to students that they are expected to have these notebooks available at every mathematics class. Some teachers develop procedures for collecting and keeping the notebooks in the classroom. This may work well, but sometimes students can benefit from reviewing their notebooks at home, particularly if they consistently write about what they are learning. The notebooks become great tools for reflection and review.

Some teachers prefer to give writing tasks on looseleaf paper, such as duplicated problem tasks or specific prompts to guide student exploration. It is still a good practice for students to organize and collect their work in a binder. One teacher who used this practice would have students complete these tasks four to five times during a typical

2-week unit. She would give the students a sheet with a problem or prompt for investigation, or sometimes a couple of questions to focus their consideration of a concept or an idea. The school's parent organization bought inexpensive clasp folders for each student, and the teacher would use three-hole paper as well as color sheets to separate assignments for different chapters. This worked well for the teacher. The folders were less bulky than notebooks and did not constitute an additional supply expense for the students. When the teacher wanted to review the folders, she found them much easier to collect than 20 or so notebooks or composition books.

Although portfolios are considered out of vogue by some, they are another option that teachers have for organizing and collecting student work (Koch & Petterson, 2000). Portfolios include a wide range of student products. Some teachers include several writing assignments as examples of student growth and progress. The portfolio process itself generally requires students to engage in some level of reflection to provide a written overview of the artifacts in the portfolio. Teachers may require specific writing tasks to be included in a student's portfolio and may also allow students to include additional pieces as examples that demonstrate what they learned or as examples of excellent work. Using portfolios as an assessment tool provides a mechanism by which teachers can include writing as part of a comprehensive picture of a student's mathematical understanding. This also allows the teacher and the student to focus on key assignments and self-selected examples of exemplary work. This promotes writing as integral to and valued in mathematical learning.

How Teachers Handle Assessment

This section will present some basic procedures that teachers have tried and modified in the assessment of students' writing in mathematics. Classroom teachers should consider these as examples and then modify them to meet their own needs. The goal is to use writing as a learning tool and to allow assessment to provide a vehicle for promoting this goal. These strategies, shared by various teachers at different grade levels, provide a way of valuing and using writing to support mathematical learning while showing how to handle assessment in ways that do not require substantive additional time commitments.

Not all writing should be assessed by the teacher. This may seem like a simple idea, but teachers frequently struggle for some sort of balance. Throughout this book the idea that writing must be viewed

as an important part of mathematics instruction has been emphasized. The teacher can set this tone while allowing for writing that is
done to promote reflection and for the student's benefit. Many teachers think that this type of writing shouldn't be collected and assessed.
If so, how do teachers communicate that this type of writing is important? Teachers have shared various means of dealing with this
issue. One teacher notes that she circulates when students are doing "free writes" and records a checkmark in the grade book as an
indicator that the students are writing. She may stop and discuss a
student's writing with him or her from time to time. The idea that
she communicates is that the writing is personal, but it must still
have substantive mathematical content.

Another teacher shared that he has students write daily in a journal and then uses about 10 minutes of class time on the last day of
the week for a synthesis paragraph. In the synthesis paragraph, the
students reread their personal entries for the week and write about
important mathematical ideas they learned or share an approach to
a problem they solved. Students are encouraged to include quotes
and paraphrases from their original writings. These synthesis paragraphs reflect a commitment to daily writing and provide students
with an opportunity to reflect on their writing and synthesize key
ideas and concepts. These synthesis paragraphs are then assessed.

Rotating Assessment

Several teachers have shared different versions of the rotating assessment system. Students write frequently in a notebook or collect
their writings in a folder. Instead of the teacher reading each folder
every day, three or four students' writing samples are collected each
day. The teacher can then focus on the students' writing and assess
the work. Teachers who have block-scheduling classes may have seven
or eight folders from each class to assess. In this system all the student writing is usually assessed once every 2 weeks. This allows
writing to continue as part of the mathematics instruction and makes
it part of the assessment routine the teacher develops. Teachers indicate that an advantage of this system is that viewing several pieces
of writing from one student gives them a better picture of what that
individual student knows about a topic. Teachers also indicate that
it is easier to see growth in a student's mathematical understanding
and mathematical communication skills when reviewing several
pieces of writing. Some teachers give an overall assessment of the
writing instead of assessing the individual assignments.

Selective Sampling

Selective sampling is considered by many teachers to be a powerful student-oriented assessment process. For each unit, students can select any piece of their writing to be assessed, and the teacher will also randomly select a task. One teacher indicated that she would select the piece before collecting the folders so that she was less likely to show bias. She would let the students know as she collected their folders that she had selected a certain task. If a student had selected that task as his or her personal choice, the teacher would use a second selected task for that student. This process gives students an opportunity to showcase their best work and provides motivation for continued good writing because students do not know which piece will be selected by the teacher. A high school teacher shared that he put a slip of paper with the tasks written on them in a box and drew a slip to indicate which writing task would be formally assessed.

Group Writing Tasks

A middle school teacher emphasized that she had students complete at least one group writing task each week. She stressed that it was important to require one written response to the task from the group. The writing was assessed formally, and each student in the group received the same grade. Because each student was expected to contribute to the process, this was accepted as fair and equitable by the students. The teacher indicated that this group writing process was productive and that students really demonstrated an understanding of key ideas. It also made assessing the writing much easier.

Rewriting a Task

An elementary school teacher shared a unique approach that underscored the writing-to-learn nature of her writing tasks. After several writing tasks had been completed by students (and kept in their composition book), she would devote class time to rewriting one task. Sometimes students would select the piece of writing. At other times, the teacher would select the task, often based on the central importance of ideas or strategies for that particular unit or because students had demonstrated some difficulty with the material. Students would use their initial writing product and work on a polished version. The teacher would circulate and assist students with the writing task. This gave her an opportunity to focus on extending ideas and concepts or on working on strategies and procedures. The final product was collected and assessed. In structuring the task in this way, the teacher could make notes about which students were writing effectively and which students needed more assistance. Drawing from the tasks that the students had previously written communicated that writing was important to learning and should be revisited and revised.

What Should Be Assessed?

The goal of assessment is best thought of in terms of assessing *for* student learning instead of assessment *of* student learning (Davies, 2000; Lim, 2004). Assessment of student writing in mathematics supports an increase in descriptive feedback that helps students to understand the mathematics that they know and how well they are doing; thus, the assessment process supports student learning. Research indicates that frequent feedback to students about their learning results in substantial learning gains (Black & William, 1998). The feedback should focus on the task, emphasizing the knowledge and skills that are relevant, and should be given in a timely manner. Refer back to the model depicting the interaction that is associated with writing and speaking mathematics (Figure 6-1). The feedback loop in that model underscores the power of writing in providing a means for students to receive information that ultimately plays a formative assessment role in guiding their learning.

Mathematics teachers who assess students' writing frequently struggle for a balance between a focus on the mathematics and a focus on the writing. It is imperative that teachers remember that the goal of writing in mathematics is to support students' understanding of mathematical ideas and concepts. This should always be the central goal for teachers of mathematics as they implement writing in their classes. Some teachers decide not to focus on grammar and mechanics. Although the content of the writing is of central importance, opportunities to help students refine their use of grammar and other conventions of language should be reinforced. Some teachers decide to not penalize students for grammar and mechanics but simply point out any errors found in the writing. Many teachers will ask students to revise a written task if it does not clearly convey a message. Previous chapters communicated the importance of writing and stressed the importance of helping students to develop standards criteria by which their writing would be evaluated. These standards are important to continually reinforce. The four elements in chapter 4 provide a framework for developing assessment procedures for students' writing.

As teachers begin to consider the mathematics (which should always be the primary emphasis in the assessment of the writing), the goals and objectives of the lesson should be considered. The writing tasks should clearly support the instructional goals of the lesson. Consider how the writing demonstrates students' (a) mathematical knowledge, (b) conceptual understanding, (c) procedural understanding, (d) problem-solving abilities, and (e) level of mathematical reasoning (Kulm, 1990). These five areas, discussed more thoroughly below, should relate directly to instruction. What students are expected to demonstrate must be a focus of the instruction. There must be an alignment between what teachers look for when assessing student work and the opportunities afforded the students during mathematics instruction. This simple principle should drive all of the teacher's assessment practices.

Mathematical Knowledge

Teachers should consider any state and local objectives or competencies that guide the decisions they make about the instruction provided. These indicators provide helpful information about the mathematics that students are expected to know. Teachers are required to consistently align their instruction with state and local curricular competencies or goals. This is important to keep in mind when providing administrators with information about writing tasks. The writing-to-learn tasks provide powerful assessment tools for identifying what students know about mathematics. Teachers should also consider the National Council of Teachers of Mathematics standards (NCTM, 2000). This document provides expectations for five content strands: numbers and operations, algebra, geometry, measurement, and data analysis and probability. These expectations (which are summarized in a table in the NCTM document) provide useful targets for teachers to consider when thinking about the mathematics that students know. Table 7-1 shows one expectation from the algebra standard for each of the grade-level bands. Although these expectations are broad, they provide a context within which teachers can think about how specific lesson objectives align with some big ideas related to students' mathematical knowledge.

Table 7-1.   Example of Algebra Expectations for Grade-Level Bands (NCTM Standards)

	Pre-K–2	Grades 3–5	Grades 6–8	Grades 9–12
Analyze change in various contexts. (Algebra instructional goal for pre-K through grade 12.)	Describe quantitative change, such as a student's growing 2 inches in 1 year.	Identify and describe situations with constant or varying rates of change and compare them.	Use graphs to analyze the nature of changes in quantities in linear relationships.	Approximate and interpret rates of change from graphical and numerical data.

Conceptual Understanding

Assessment of conceptual understanding of mathematics is made attainable with writing. Traditional assessments frequently lack the attention to detail that is necessary to obtain information about students' conceptual understanding of mathematics topics. Conceptual understanding focuses on knowing *about* something. It means knowing that $1/2$ multiplied by $1/4$ means that taking $1/4$ of the $1/2$ results in $1/8$ of the total. Students with conceptual understanding can reason and apply mathematics. Writing often requires students to tell why something works; thus, the process of writing helps them to learn mathematics at a deeper level, and the writing provides a means of assessing what students really know about a topic or idea.

Procedural Understanding

Procedural understanding is related to skills development. It involves knowing *how* to do something. It means knowing how to multiply $1/2$ by $1/4$ to get $1/8$, but not necessarily knowing why it works or how it connects to other mathematical ideas. Teachers should work to develop students' procedural understanding and conceptual understanding simultaneously (National Research Council, 2001). The Mathematical Sciences Education Board (1993) uses an analogy of assessing writing to make a point about assessing procedural and conceptual knowledge. Assessment of good writing focuses on grammar, spelling, and vocabulary as well as engaging students in writing sentences, paragraphs, and essays. Mathematics too should focus on students' involvement with solving problems, making conjectures, and formulating convincing arguments. Assessment of procedural understanding can easily be achieved through evaluating students' selection and implementation of procedures when they are engaged in doing mathematics. Writing provides the tool that gives students an opportunity to reflect and describe the strategies and methods that they are using. This provides a useful means by which the teacher can understand why students select various paths in completing mathematical tasks; thus, the information gained provides more precise indicators of those procedures that students have actually mastered. Research indicates that focusing on problem solving helps students to learn both concepts and skills, and that students with limited or low levels of conceptual understanding require additional practice in order to develop procedural knowledge (Grouws & Cebulla, 2000). These levels of understanding can be assessed through students' writing, providing teachers with information to help students develop mathematical literacy.

Problem-Solving Abilities

Some mathematicians would argue that mathematics is problem solving. Problem solving is definitely the heart of mathematics, but assessing mathematical problem-solving capabilities can be difficult for teachers. Problem solving involves the application of prior knowledge and skills to resolve a situation that lacks an apparent solution. Writing provides clear evidence of what students can do relative to selecting and implementing effective problem-solving processes. Table 7-2 lists several key areas to consider when assessing students' problem-solving behaviors. There are four primary phases that characterize students' actions during mathematical problem solving: orientation, organization, execution, and verification. Subcategories for each of these phases provide more refined levels for viewing how students perform various problem-solving actions (Pugalee, 2004). Teachers can use student writing to gain insight into how they approach and carry out mathematical problem solving. Using a framework is valuable because it provides information about precise problems that students may face in solving mathematics problems. Writing becomes a tool for understanding where and how students' problem-solving attempts encounter difficulty.

Table 7-2.   Framework for Assessing Problem-Solving Behaviors

Orientation	Organization	Execution	Verification
Reading/Rereading Initial/Subsequent Representation Analysis of Information & Conditions Assessment of Difficulty	Identification of Goals Making & Implementing Plans Data Organization	Performing Goals Monitoring Goals Calculations Redirecting	Evaluating Decisions Checking Calculations

Mathematical Reasoning

NCTM (2000) asserts that being able to reason is essential to mathematical understanding. Reasoning involves developing ideas, exploring phenomena, justifying results, and using mathematical conjectures. Writing allows students to demonstrate their level of mathematical reasoning. Teachers at different grade levels will require various degrees of sophistication in what is considered appropriate mathematical reasoning for their particular students. Teachers should consider students' writing for evidence of how they do the following:

1. Draw logical conclusions about mathematics
2. Use models, known facts, properties, and relationships to explain their thinking
3. Justify their answers and solution processes
4. Use patterns and relationships to analyze mathematical situations
5. Communicate a belief that mathematics makes sense

These five areas provide an approach for understanding how students reason about mathematics. Writing provides a tool not only for assessing students' mathematical reasoning but also for promoting the development of higher order thinking processes that are indicative of accomplished levels of mathematical reasoning.

Managing Feedback

Writing comments on papers can be a labor-intensive project. Feedback is important because it extends a discussion with the student. The goal of providing feedback is to improve student learning. Comments written on students' papers will benefit the student if he or she has an opportunity to improve the writing or to better demonstrate mathematical understanding. Although the premise for providing written comments is laudable, research indicates that students rarely use summative or final written comments to improve their writing (Harris, 1979; Wiltse, 2002). Assessment appears to be more beneficial to students if they have opportunities to respond to the feedback. There are several ways to manage feedback without writing extensive comments on students' papers:

1. Identify key strengths and weaknesses and address these with the entire class. The goal is to improve students' mathematical writing, and general issues will help students to understand good practices and look out for problem areas.

2. While monitoring students' work that involves writing, make comments and ask questions to guide writing as students are working on their tasks.

3. Use examples of good writing to show to the entire class as a way of reinforcing and developing common performance expectations about written products.

4. Use peer and group assessment. Students can effectively identify and specify strengths and weaknesses in writing.

5. Limit written comments and focus questions or comments so they will guide writing.

The next chapter will provide more information on how students can work together to analyze and provide feedback about peers' mathematical writing.

Applying the Assessment Process

The following discussion focuses on a piece of writing produced in a second-grade mathematics classroom following a lesson on perimeter and area. The discussion will focus on the four elements of good writing and the five key mathematical areas discussed on p. 117. Keep in mind that a classroom in which good writing is valued and high expectations communicated will result in a high student awareness of good writing.

In Figure 7-1, second-grade students were asked to find the amount of fence that would be needed to enclose a field for some animals if the field is 10 feet by 6 feet.

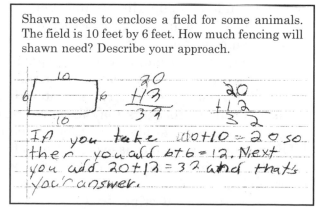

Shawn needs to enclose a field for some animals. The field is 10 feet by 6 feet. How much fencing will shawn need? Describe your approach.

Figure 7-1. Second-Grade Perimeter Task

First, briefly consider the four elements of good writing as a framework for thinking about the quality of the student's written response to the task.

Does the writing express a clear purpose? Although there is a clear purpose implied through the student's response, the student doesn't state a specific goal. For many teachers this is not problematic, because the prompt provides a clear indication of the purpose of the writing. This student goes directly into describing his approach. Teachers may want to address this with their students. Formal assessments of writing most often require a clear statement about the purpose of the writing. Teachers may consider having students begin with an introductory statement about what it is that they are trying to accomplish. For example, a student could have written an opening statement about needing to find the distance around the field. Restating the prompt in this fashion also helps students to focus their thinking.

Does the structure and development provide details, arguments, justifications, and assertions that lead to a conclusion? This paper clearly provides details, including a diagram, supporting the student's answer. The student understands that the dimensions of the field will be the same on opposite sides. He adds the two longer sides and then the two shorter sides. These two sums are then added together to get the total distance around the field and the amount of fence needed. The student confidently describes how he added the dimensions, including labeling the diagram and showing computations.

Are information and ideas conveyed in a precise and concise manner? The student approaches the task in a very systematic fashion. The writing specifies clear procedures for finding the perimeter of the field. The diagram and computations provide important background information about what the student is doing. The writing doesn't include any superfluous information or ideas. At more advanced levels, students might be expected to connect their response to their diagrams and computations.

Are basic grammar and mechanics evident? The student responds in complete sentences. The main error is the apostrophe in *you'r,* but this level of accuracy for emerging writers is considered acceptable by most teachers. Teachers may focus on grammar and mechanics that are expected for students at their grade level.

The primary goal of our assessment is to focus on the mathematical understanding of the student. The five key mathematical areas listed earlier provide a useful framework for considering the mathematics in students' writing.

What mathematical knowledge is reflected in the student's writing? The student shows in his writing that he can develop a plan for finding the perimeter of a rectangle. His use of diagrams shows that he understands that rectangular areas have opposite sides that are the same length. These are key mathematical concepts for students to understand.

What is the student's level of conceptual understanding? The student shows a solid understanding of the concept of perimeter. The diagram drawn by the student helps to clarify what he knows about perimeter and rectangles. From his writing, including the diagram and computations, it is evident that he understands perimeter as the distance around an object, although the precise term *perimeter* isn't used.

Does the student demonstrate procedural understanding? The student's addition of opposite sides of the rectangle and his discussion of these actions in his written statement indicate that he is comfortable with these operations. His pairing of 10 and 10 and then 6 and 6 shows that he is using efficient procedures for finding sums. There are no errors in the execution of the algorithms and appropriate algorithms, are selected during the problem solving.

Does the student use sound problem solving? The writing provides a window into how the student thought about the problem. He devised and executed a plan for finding the distance around the field. He applied several steps to reach this goal. He used verification procedures to consider the reasonableness of the final answer, as evidenced in his repetition of the addition of 20 and 12.

What is the students' level of mathematical reasoning? Mathematical reasoning is evident in how the student clearly and concisely developed his ideas. The student was able to justify results and used a diagram to support his computations. He demonstrates that he understands that rectangles have opposite sides that are equal. Older students might be expected to use more technical mathematical language such as *rectangle* and *perimeter*. Overall, the student demonstrates solid and focused reasoning that leads to a correct solution.

Summary

This chapter provided some general guidelines about managing students' writing. Time and material considerations included some strategies for helping teachers to organize and manage keeping up with more student papers. Assessment that is time efficient was an important part of this discussion. Specific strategies shared by classroom teachers that promote both the efficiency and effectiveness of assessing students writing were provided. What to assess was a major focus of the chapter. Assessment was discussed in the context of the four elements of good writing discussed in chapter 4. Additionally, five domains for mathematical understanding were offered. These five domains, along with the four elements of good writing, were applied to a piece of student writing dealing with perimeter to demonstrate how these components could provide a solid approach in assessing mathematical understanding and their general writing abilities.

Developing Rubrics
and Assessment Procedures

Important ideas about good writing in mathematics have been developed, but these characteristics are not easily assessed without the consideration of multiple criteria, such as elements of composing and substantive mathematical concepts and ideas. Students' written products provide teachers with an opportunity to assess a wide range of skills and knowledge, yet assessment of writing requires an approach that differs from traditional methods of assessment. The complex nature of the information that mathematical writing provides requires an assessment process that describes levels of performance for multiple components. Rubrics provide such a tool. This chapter will develop key ideas about the development of rubrics and demonstrate how they can be used effectively as assessment tools by mathematics teachers and students.

The Nature of Rubrics and Assessment

Assessment is a complex process. The assessment principle from the NCTM (2000) standards specifies that teachers need to understand mathematical goals deeply, understand how students are thinking about mathematics, and be skilled in interpreting assessment information. A rubric provides direction for a teacher in assessing tasks or learning activities by specifying and describing standards that help him or her to make decisions about student performance.

Rubrics provide indicators of student performance. They help to direct instruction because they provide the teacher with concrete ideas about what student performance should look like; thus, teachers can develop instruction that helps students to reach maximal performance levels. Analytic rubrics can help teachers to identify students' strengths and weaknesses, thus becoming an important dynamic feedback loop between assessment and instruction. In addition, students find rubrics useful in self-assessment. Because the rubrics are aligned to performance expectations, students have a better idea of how their performance will be assessed.[1]

There are two common types of rubrics: analytic and holistic. Both serve important assessment functions. An *analytic rubric* identifies and describes the components of a product or an outcome (such as the Rubric for Assessing the Five Mathematical Areas, presented later in this chapter). A *holistic rubric* describes the product or outcome as a whole (such as the general rubric for Open-Ended Assessment, presented in chapter 9). Teachers will need to consider which rubric best meets their assessment goals. Both types of rubrics might be used at different times for various assignments or tasks. Holistic rubrics are sometimes preferred for younger children or for students who have little experience with rubrics as an assessment tool. The holistic rubric doesn't have the level of detail found in the analytic rubric. Analytic rubrics provide sufficient detail to allow teachers to differentiate performance on multiple components. This differentiation is represented by scales or levels.

Regardless of the type of rubric used, it is important to model the use of the rubric with examples of products and tasks so that students understand how the rubric is to be interpreted. Some teachers within a particular school might adopt a common rubric so that assessment is more uniform throughout the school; this is often a popular approach among specific grade-level and content area teachers.

A question that always arises is how rubrics can be used when students must eventually receive a letter grade. Individual teachers will handle this situation in different ways. Some schools might have a policy that gives direction. The levels on rubrics do not necessarily correspond to letter grades, and tasks or assignments that are evaluated with a rubric account for only one type of information that the teacher has about student performance. The ideas offered here are intended to be thinking points to help teachers address this question. One thing to consider is what the various performance levels mean. Generally, the lowest level, which typically includes all F and some D students, is unacceptable. The highest level, which includes A and B students, is indicative of exemplary performance. Many teachers decide to include only A and B+ students here. That leaves one or two middle level(s) to represent students who are still working toward proficiency. C students fit into one of these levels or might span the two levels, depending on teacher preference. Some teachers use plus and minus systems to provide additional information about where a student's work fits using the rubric.

Teachers may also weigh different parts of a rubric and develop a point system. Brookhart (2004) and Nitko (2001) suggest the development of a rubric corresponding to performance required for A, B, C, D, and F letter grades. The rubric must describe the performance at each grade level. Teachers should also decide what percentage of a student's grade will come from tasks assessed using rubrics. A procedure specifying how rubrics will be used in determining grades must be developed and communicated to students and parents.

Constructing the Rubrics

Constructing a rubric doesn't have to be a difficult process. There are many good resources available with examples and other information. A search on the Internet will bring up numerous sites that provide not only information but also generators to help construct rubrics. The general guidelines that follow provide a beginning point for the construction of rubrics. Once rubrics are constructed, teachers can refine and reuse them.

- Identify the concepts or skills to be assessed. Objectives and instructional goals provide useful guidelines.
- Identify levels of performance from low to high, using either descriptors or numerical scales.
- Identify the criteria to be assessed and develop descriptors for each level that differentiate and characterize what performance should look like for each criterion. (Holistic models will not specify individual criteria but will still need to provide global descriptors that differentiate the performance levels.)
- The rubric should be tested with student samples and revised as necessary before final implementation.

Describing specific criteria that distinguish performance at different levels is the most difficult part of constructing effective rubrics. This process will be demonstrated in the following pages by developing a possible rubric for assessing the mathematical content of students' writing. A five-scale rubric will be developed. Teachers who want to align the rubric to roughly correspond to letter-grade performance can refine the levels to do so.

This sample analytic rubric doesn't necessarily align with letter-grade expectations. It includes dimensions for each of the five mathematics components that are important in assessing students' writing, as identified in the previous chapter.

Skills and Concepts

In Chapter 7, five key mathematical areas were described: (a) mathematical knowledge—key ideas and concepts from mathematics content, (b) conceptual understanding—understanding and reasoning in applying mathematics, (c) procedural understanding—carrying our procedures and algorithms successfully, (d) problem-solving abilities—development and execution of a plan for solving a problem, and (e) level of mathematical reasoning—developing ideas and conjectures with supporting mathematical justification. These five areas will serve as a framework for developing a rubric that assesses each one at various performance levels, but our discussion will focus on mathematical knowledge and conceptual understanding. These skills and concepts will be demonstrated with varying levels of sophistication. The rubric developed here is a framework for demonstrating the process; however, the rubric can be refined to suit individual situations.

Levels

This rubric will utilize five levels, from 0 to 4:

0: Unsatisfactory work or work that demonstrates lack of minimal competency; little or no evidence of criteria.

1: Beginning or demonstration of some knowledge or skills related to criteria, but needs significant improvement.

2: Development or demonstration of knowledge or skills at a level that needs improvement; partially meets criteria.

3: Accomplished; demonstrates knowledge and skills at a satisfactory level (as determined by classroom and/or other academic expectations) with no identifiable problems.

4: Mastery; demonstrates extended knowledge and skills at an exemplary level.

Specifying these levels provides a beginning point to describe specific performance criteria for each learning target. At this stage, it is helpful to obtain numerous student products that illustrate a wide range of performance. Going through the students' work and grouping it into these broad performance levels will provide a springboard for specifying the criteria for each level. A guiding question is "How are the student responses at this level different from those in other levels?" (Nitko, 2001).

Criteria

Identifying the criteria is the heart of the rubric. Specific descriptors must be shaped that concisely yet informatively describe the behaviors that are indicative of performance at that level. In addition, there must be differentiation between the descriptions at each of the grade levels. This step frequently requires several revisions before it is acceptable. Even after these criteria are written, they should be revisited from time to time within the context of the instructional goals and revised in order to more precisely reflect teacher expectations.

This process will be demonstrated for mathematical content and conceptual understanding. Both of these are complex learning targets, and teachers might have slightly different indicators or levels of specificity depending on their particular learning goals. The criteria described in this rubric (Table 8-1) are provided as a guideline. There is no reason to reinvent the wheel, but existing rubrics should always be carefully reviewed and revised to correspond to the curriculum and the instructional goals of the teacher. Good criteria should be concise, avoid unnecessary descriptors, describe observable characteristics, and be written in clearly understood language. To develop the criteria, general descriptors of skills and concepts and samples of student work for each level were used to guide the process of specifying what performance at each level should look like. In addition, objectives and curricular goals that serve as the framework for teaching and learning provided useful references for considering what is important and how the language might best be worded.

Table 8-1. Rubric for Mathematical Content and Conceptual Understanding

Level	Mathematical Content	Conceptual Understanding
4	The mathematics is accurate. All mathematical concepts and ideas are accurately identified. Mathematical terms are used appropriately.	Gives support for major concepts, supplies examples with explanations when appropriate.
3	The mathematics is accurate. Most mathematical concepts and ideas are accurately identified. Mathematical terms are used appropriately, but there may be minor errors.	Gives support for major concepts but may omit minor details. May use examples when appropriate but may not effectively relate example to mathematical concepts.
2	The mathematics contains minor errors. Mathematical concepts and ideas are identified but may contain minor errors. There are notable errors in the use of mathematical terms.	Gives support for major concepts but may have minor errors in logic or understanding. Minor details are ignored or supported with incorrect or flawed thinking.
1	The mathematics is mostly inaccurate. Mathematical concepts and ideas are identified with several errors. Mathematical terms are used inappropriately.	Attempts are made to support major concepts, but there are errors in logic or understanding.
0	No answer, or mathematics has no relationship to the task.	No attempts are made to support major concepts, or major concepts are not appropriately identified.

In focusing on mathematical content, several indicators emerge from a review of standards documents such as NCTM's (2000) *Principles and Standards for School Mathematics,* state curricular frameworks, and samples of student work. "What is important to consider when identifying what students know about the mathematics content?" became the guiding question for developing criteria. First, solid understanding of mathematical content will be evident through the identification of mathematical concepts and ideas that are central to the task or problem. Second, the correctness of the mathematics in the response goes beyond just a correct answer to include all the different mathematics concepts and skills reflected in the problem or task. Third, the student's use of terminology relates to properly identifying major mathematical concepts and being able to use proper terminology throughout the response. Performance levels reflect how student products might demonstrate clear differences in their level of mathematical content knowledge.

Conceptual knowledge extends the consideration of mathematical content knowledge. The primary consideration is the degree to which students can provide information about the mathematical concepts that are important in the problem. This goes beyond identifying a concept appropriately to connecting that concept to the task or problem. Does the student show that he or she fully understands the mathematical concepts that are inherent in the problem or task? The use of examples and illustrations is considered a hallmark of students who have a deeper level of conceptual understanding.

In considering the complete rubric (Table 8-2), one will note that there are similarities in the criteria for several of the mathematical areas. For example, conceptual understanding and mathematical reasoning both deal with assessing how students' writing reveals a deeper understanding of the mathematics being used. They are interrelated. Students with a deep conceptual understanding are likely to exhibit sound reasoning, which is more concerned with how students defend and justify their actions, whereas conceptual understanding focuses more on identifying and describing the mathematics in the problem. The nature of mathematical understanding draws on these multiple dimensions, and they are not easily brought out and described as discrete factors. Teachers and other professionals will need practice applying such rubrics so that the criteria become clear. Many teachers prefer to use holistic rubrics instead of analytic rubrics because they are easier to apply and easier for students to understand.

Table 8-2. Rubric for Assessing the Five Mathematical Areas

Level	Mathematical Content	Conceptual Understanding	Procedural Understanding	Problem Solving Ability	Mathematical Reasoning
4	The mathematics is accurate. All mathematical concepts and ideas are accurately identified. Mathematical terms are used appropriately.	The mathematics is accurate. All mathematical concepts and ideas are accurately identified. Mathematical terms are used appropriately.	Selects and executes appropriate strategies. Representations and algorithms are appropriate.	Identifies the goal of the problem or task. Develops a plan that shows an understanding of all components of the problem. Plan is executed with no errors.	Completely and accurately provides justification for major steps or processes. Defends reasonableness of answer with supporting reasons.
3	The mathematics is accurate. Mathematical concepts and ideas are accurately identified. Mathematical terms are used appropriately, but there may be minor errors.	The mathematics is accurate. Most mathematical concepts and ideas are accurately identified. Mathematical terms are used appropriately, but there may be minor errors.	Selects and executes appropriate strategies. Representations and algorithms may have minor errors but do not affect the solution.	Identifies the goal of the problem or task. Develops a plan that shows an understanding of the problem but may contain minor errors in executing the plan.	Accurately provides justification for major steps or processes but lacks clarity or detail. Defends reasonableness of answer but may have minor omissions or errors in describing approach.

(Continued)

Table 8-2.   Rubric for Assessing the Five Mathematical Areas *(Continued)*

Level	Mathematical Content	Conceptual Understanding	Procedural Understanding	Problem Solving Ability	Mathematical Reasoning
2	The mathematics contains minor errors. Mathematical concepts and ideas are identified but with minor errors. There are notable errors in the use of mathematical terms.	The mathematics contains minor errors. Mathematical concepts and ideas are identified but may contain minor errors. There are notable errors in the use of mathematical terms.	Selects appropriate approach, but execution is flawed. Representations and algorithms may be appropriate for the task but are not executed properly.	Identifies the goal of the problem or task but misinterprets one or more components of the problem. Plan indicates minimal understanding of problem.	Provides justification for most of the steps or processes with no errors. Defends reasonableness of answer but may not develop supporting reasons.
1	The mathematics is mostly inaccurate. Mathematical concepts and ideas are identified with several errors. Mathematical terms are used inappropriately.	The mathematics is mostly inaccurate. Mathematical concepts and ideas are identified with several errors. Mathematical terms are used inappropriately.	Selects an inappropriate approach or selects the appropriate approach but cannot begin implementation. Representations and algorithms are not appropriate for the task.	Does not identify the goal of the problem or task, but response shows some evidence of understanding the general nature of the problem. Does not develop a plan.	Provides some justification for steps or processes but contains numerous errors. Limited or no supporting evidence defending reasonableness of answer.
0	No answer, or mathematics has no relationship to the task.	No answer, or mathematics has no relationship to the task.	No evidence of representations or algorithms that would indicate an acceptable approach.	No evidence of understanding the goal of the task or problem. No attempt to specify or develop a plan.	Does not attempt to provide any justification for steps or processes.

Applying the Rubrics

Three examples of student work—one each from elementary, middle, and secondary school—will be used to illustrate how the completed rubric can be applied. In chapter 7 the four elements of good writing were discussed, along with an example of assessing the quality of those elements. A holistic rubric incorporating these four elements is provided (Table 8-3) and applied to these written products. Teachers may prefer to construct an analytic rubric that describes criteria for each of the four elements at the various levels of performance.

Table 8-3.   Rubric for Assessing the Four Elements of Writing

Level	Criteria
4	The writing reflects a clear goal. The writing is well organized, with details and arguments leading to a conclusion; sequencing is effective and connections are clear. There is good detail, with descriptions using clear and precise language that supports major mathematical ideas or actions; mathematical vocabulary is appropriately used throughout the response. Consistently applies acceptable use of grammar and mechanics.
3	The writing reflects a goal but may not be stated clearly. The writing is well organized, with details and arguments leading to a conclusion; sequencing is effective but some connections are not clear. There is good detail and descriptions using clear and precise language that supports major mathematical ideas or actions, but a few minor details might be vague; writing might not reflect consistent use of mathematical vocabulary. Might have minor grammatical or mechanical errors.
2	The writing does not state a goal, but a purpose is reflected in the response. The writing has some organization, but the details and arguments are confusing; sequencing is evident but may be confusing. Detail and descriptions are minimal but do support major mathematical ideas; a few minor details might be missing; writing might not reflect consistent use of mathematical vocabulary, or one or two terms might be used inappropriately. Might have several minor grammatical or mechanical errors.
1	The writing does not have a clear goal. There is little organization evident, with details and arguments vague or nonexistent. Detail and descriptions are vague or absent; mathematical vocabulary is basically nonexistent or mostly incorrect. Paper has major grammatical or mechanical errors.
0	No attempt to respond to the task, or the attempt is confusing and inaccurate. Contains major grammatical or mechanical errors.

First-Grade Example

Figure 8-1 demonstrates how writing can help teachers to understand students' thinking about computation problems.

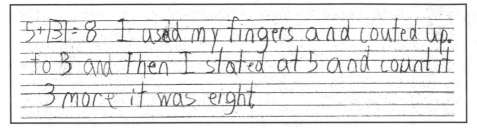

5 + [3] = 8 I used my fingers and counted up to 3 and then I stated at 5 and count it 3 more it was eight

Figure 8-1. First-Grade Description of Addition Problem

The mathematical content rating for this piece is 4. The student demonstrates an understanding of counting and uses terminology appropriate for this level such as "3 more." The problem reinforces the student's understanding of addition and basic number facts. He can also read and write the numbers appropriately.

The conceptual understanding rating is also 4. Counting is a foundation for young students' understanding numbers. This student demonstrates that he understands that the next numbers in the counting sequence will give him the missing addend. He effectively describes how he would use the total number of fingers (8), counting from 5 and keeping track of the additional three counts to arrive at 8. The student understands the concept of addition. He also demonstrates a basic understanding of equality. The student shows that he understands the relationship between 5 + ___ on the left side of the equal sign and 8 on the right side. This is an important foundation in developing algebraic thinking.[2]

For procedural understanding, the response receives a score of 4. The student selects appropriate procedures for finding the answer. He uses "counting on 5" to find out how much is needed to get to 8. Counting on and counting back are important procedures for finding sums and differences.

For problem solving, the product receives a score of 4. The student expresses a goal for finding the answer: "I used my fingers and counted up." He then effectively executes this plan. Students at higher grade levels may be expected to be more explicit in stating the goal of the problem or task. Teachers must exercise their professional judgment in determining what is acceptable for the criteria used to delineate performance for the various mathematical areas.

The student's response receives a score of 3 on mathematical reasoning. The teacher thought that the student could have provided more detail justifying the answer. The student did an excellent job of explaining how he arrived at the answer, but there was no detail that would show extended mathematical reasoning abilities. For a score of 4, the teacher expected some level of justification for a correct solution, perhaps an illustration or a drawing. Students had worked extensively with subtraction, and that operation could have been related to the problem. The student had previously demonstrated proficiency with addition and subtraction facts up to 20.

Now let's apply the rubric designed to assess the quality of students' writing based on the four elements of good writing. Here the student would receive a rating of 3. Although a goal is not specifically articulated, the response reflects the tacit goal of focusing on the target equation of 5 + 3 = 8. The student not only explained a strategy for solving the problem—"I used my fingers and cou[n]ted up to 3"—but also included a specific sequence within the strategy "then I started at 5 and count[ed] 3 more." Although the student did not use mathematical content-specific vocabulary (i.e., *equation, add, sum, equals*), the mathematical ideas of adding separate sets of numbers into a collective sum are described in detail.

The final criterion on the rubric is designed to assess the mechanics or grammatical elements of student writing. An analysis of the writing sample reveals a total of five grammatical or mechanical errors (*couted* for counted; *up* for up; *stated* for started; *count it* for counted; *it* for It). However, a caveat must be extended in the use of any rubric that incorporates the mechanics of writing, especially with respect to the written products of beginning readers and writers (Douville, 2000). First, an initial draft of any written product should always focus on the clear communication of ideas. As such, a first draft of a written product should be conceptualized by teachers as a piece of unfinished writing (Graves, 1994). If subsequent drafts are completed, the instructional focus should be placed on helping students to expand and clarify their ideas. Mechanics and grammar should represent a focus only in the final drafts of a product that result in a piece of finished writing. However, much student writing, especially in mathematics, focuses on "writing to learn" (Tompkins, 2003) and thus remains at the unfinished level, with an emphasis on the effective communication of ideas rather than on grammar and mechanics. Beginning readers and writers are also still in the process of learning the mechanics of language and typically are not yet able to independently apply standard spelling and grammar to written products. Consequently, the developmental level of the student must be taken into consideration when assessing the criterion of mechanics and grammar in written products.

Sixth-Grade Example

Figure 8-2 deals with combinations. Students had studied in a previous unit that the number of combinations can be found by multiplying the number of items from which one can select. This concept becomes a foundation for the later study of permutations and combinations. This particular student's response was selected to demonstrate how the rubric can be used to assess work that doesn't provide much detail. The problem given was "A car is available in four colors: green, red, blue, or black. A convertible top is available in white, tan, or black. How many color combinations are possible?"

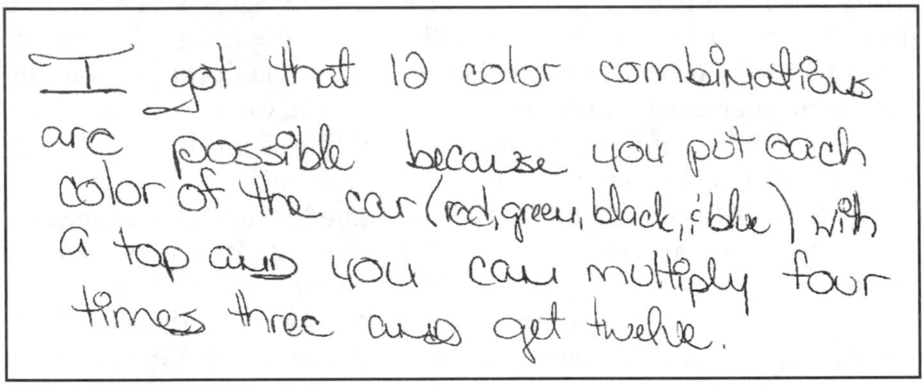

I got that 12 color combinations are possible because you put each color of the car (red, green, black, & blue) with a top and you can multiply four times three and get twelve.

Figure 8-2. Sixth-Grade Combinations Problem

For mathematical content, the response receives a 4. The mathematical content is combinations, and the student demonstrates that she understands that this involves multiplying the number of car colors by the number of top colors. Other teachers may have given this student a 2 if there was an expectation that technical terminology should be used, such as specifying that the multiplication principle would be applied to find the number of combinations.

For conceptual understanding, the response receives a 3. Combinations involve pairings, and this student demonstrates that she understands that "you put each color of the car . . . with a top." She points out that pairing the colors of the cars with a top is an effective way of finding the combinations. This is not developed fully, and there is not enough evidence to know if the student really understands how this procedure is related to the multiplication principle.

For procedural understanding, the response receives a 4. The student executes the procedure effectively. She selects multiplication as the appropriate algorithm for solving the problem. Though not elaborate, the written response indicates a solid understanding of how to use this procedure to find all the combinations for a simple two-step event.

The response receives a 4 on problem-solving ability. Some teachers may rate this area differently because the student really specifies two approaches for solving the problem. However, either plan would lead to a correct solution and the student carries out the plan of multiplying 4 and 3 to get 12. Students might be expected to fully describe multiple approaches if they are introduced in the response. Specifying a correct approach for a task is an important skill for students to develop. This student recognized the type or nature of the task as being a combinations problem, specified an approach for finding the combinations, and executed the plan effectively.

For mathematical reasoning, the response receives a 3. The major shortcoming is the student's lack of justification for using the multiplication principle. The student doesn't specify that she is using an accepted procedure for finding the number of combinations. The student should have also explained more fully how pairing the colors of the car body with the colors of the top would work. A tree diagram or other type of representation would have been sufficient. At a more advanced level, the student would have been expected to develop the relationship between the two approaches introduced in her short response.

In the writing rubric, the response receives a score of 2. The purpose is reflected in the paper but not explicitly stated. "I got that 12 color combinations are possible" shows that she has a goal for writing a description of her problem-solving processes. There is organization but there is no connection between the pairing of the body colors with the top colors and the multiplication procedure that is offered. Detail and descriptions are minimal but do support the major mathematical ideas. The student uses one long sentence to describe her approach. It is helpful for students to receive this kind of feedback about their writing so that weaknesses can be addressed in later work. This feedback can support better communication in mathematics while also helping the student to develop better writing skills in general.

High School Example

In this algebra II problem (Figure 8-3), students were asked to "Describe a process for graphing this function." The class had spent considerable time discussing the relationship between the symbolic representation of the function and the graphic representation, including using a graphing calculator and sketching graphs by hand. The teacher's expectation was that students would describe a process other than generating a table of points for the function. Although students could use the graphing calculator, they needed to describe how important points for the function could be determined from their understanding of the vertex and the x- and y-intercepts.

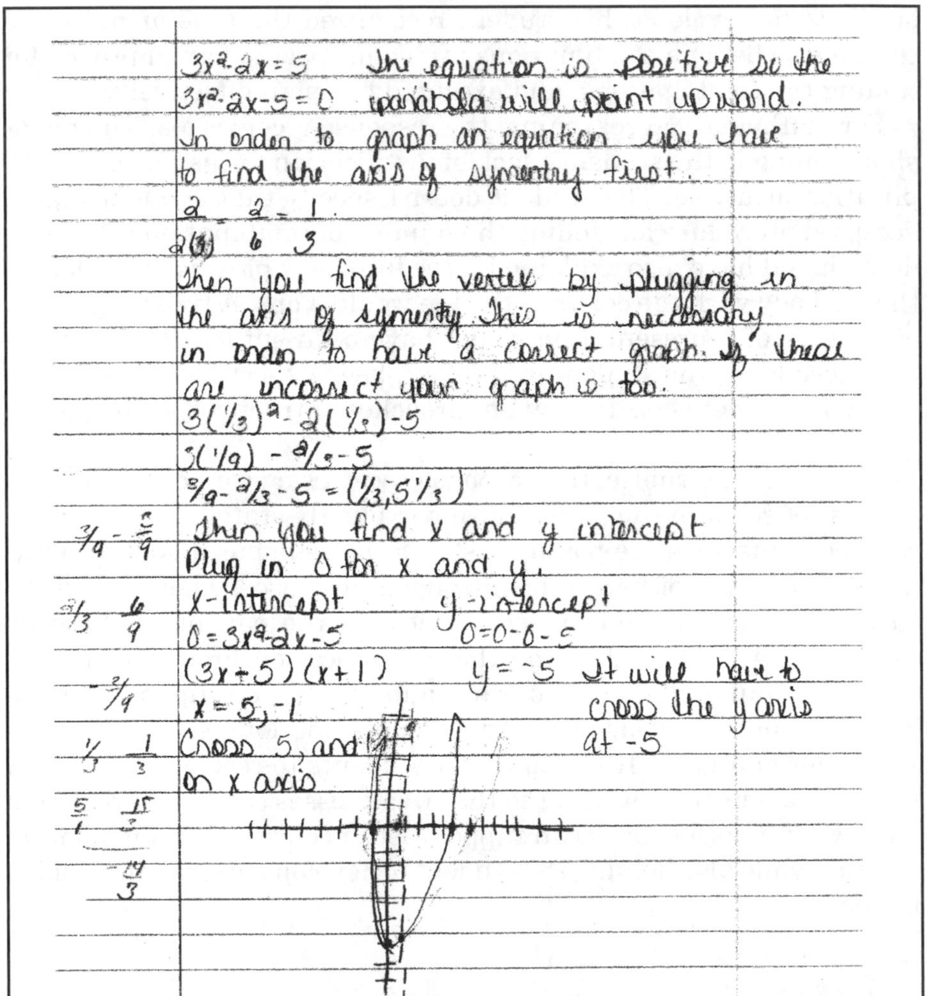

3x²-2x=5 The equation is positive so the
3x²-2x-5=0 parabola will point upward.
In order to graph an equation you have
to find the axis of symmetry first.
2/2(3) = 2/6 = 1/3
Then you find the vertex by plugging in
the axis of symmetry. This is necessary
in order to have a correct graph. If these
are incorrect your graph is too.
3(1/3)²-2(1/3)-5
3(1/9) - 2/3 - 5
3/9 - 2/3 - 5 = (1/3, 5 1/3)
Then you find x and y intercept
Plug in 0 for x and y.
x-intercept y-intercept
0=3x²-2x-5 0=0-0-5
(3x+5)(x+1) y=-5 It will have to
x=5,-1 cross the y axis
Cross 5, and -1 at -5
on x axis

Figure 8-3. Algebra II Graph of Parabola Problem

For mathematical content, the response receives a rating of 3. The student does a very good job, but there are minor problems. First, the axis of symmetry isn't properly identified as x = $^1/_3$. The teacher may have been flexible with this minor omission if the graph of the equation was more precise. Although the student correctly identifies key points, including the vertex of the graph, the vertex point is not graphed appropriately. From the student's sketch, the vertex appears to be the y-intercept instead of the vertex point ($^1/_3$, 5 $^1/_3$).

For conceptual understanding, the response receives a 4. Despite the minor error with the graph, the student does an exceptional job of identifying important features of the graph. She demonstrates an understanding of how the information obtained from various procedures can be used to graph the function. Although the graph has an error, there is strong evidence that the student can supply conceptual ideas relating the symbolic notation of a function with specific features of the graph.

For procedural understanding, the response receives a rating of 3. This illustrates how the five mathematical areas are related. If there are mathematical content errors, they will often show up again in how a student executes a particular procedure. Although she demonstrates procedural knowledge in using processes to identify the axis of symmetry, the vertex, and the x- and y-intercepts, there is a discrepancy between the graph and this information. Particularly because students can use graphing calculators at any time, there may be an expectation that greater care will be used by verifying the sketch with one obtained by using a graphing calculator.

For problem solving, the response will also receive a rating of 3. For the same reasons as identified in the above paragraph, the response is not at the exemplary level that characterizes a 4 rating. The student did develop a plan for completing the task and executed most of the steps of that plan. An important step in the plan, however, was to use the information obtained to sketch a graph. Some teachers may begin to feel uncomfortable that similar errors become a deciding factor in rating performance on several of the mathematical areas; however, these areas are difficult to separate as discrete components. Mathematical literacy involves using these interdependent processes in approaching mathematical problems.

For mathematical reasoning, the response receives a 3. The student describes her computational and procedural actions. There are no key components missing. Teachers will have to make professional judgments about the extent to which the problem with the graph of the vertex point will impact the rating. Some individuals may think that the student didn't consider the reasonableness of her responses, or she would have realized that the vertex point was not the extreme point of the sketched graph. One of the goals of mathematical reasoning is to promote reflection so that students uncover such errors. Others may believe that the problem is more procedural in nature, since the student did accurately use information from the function to identify the point.

The quality of the writing receives a rating of 3. The writing does reflect a goal, although it can be argued that the goal isn't explicitly stated. There is a very systematic process with clear connections. The student identifies the axis of symmetry, then the vertex, and then the x- and y-intercepts. There is good detail about how each is found. The student relates the information to the graph in a clear way, such as stating where the graph will cross the x axis and the y axis. "It will have to cross the y axis at –5" does not end with a period. Teachers may develop a policy of allowing students to correct minor writing errors even if the piece is a final product.

Summary

Rubrics are an effective tool for assessing students' writing in mathematics. Rubrics provide a framework for identifying important information about mathematical understanding and mathematical communication. Classroom rubrics might be viewed as works in progress, given that they should be reviewed and revised in light of the tasks to which they will be applied. A process for developing rubrics was demonstrated in specifying how mathematical content, conceptual understanding, procedural understanding, problem solving and reasoning could be assessed through students' writing. Applying this rubric, as well as a holistic writing rubric, demonstrated that there are some issues to consider. The five mathematical areas identified and described are interrelated, and there will likely be overlap (a snowballing effect, as one teacher put it) in the effect of errors on performance in more than one of these areas. Rubrics, however, still provide a sound tool for helping teachers to identify the level of students' understanding of important mathematical concepts—information that is typically not available at this level of detail through traditional assessment practices.

Notes

1. Few research studies are available that focus on rubrics. Existing studies show that instructional rubrics can help students to write better, but additional intervention, such as focusing on self-assessment, is necessary to help students perform consistently at higher levels. Studies also note gender differences, with girls responding more favorably to self-assessment. Teachers should consider cognitive and emotional responses to assessment, particularly self-assessment, related to the use of rubrics. More information is available through the Rubrics and Self-Assessment Project from Project Zero, available online at http://pzweb.harvard.edu/Research/RubricSelf.htm.

2. Algorithmic thinking as well as the development of number sense are important foundations for developing algebraic thinking. Driscoll (1999) encourages teachers to capitalize on the thinking of students by "making the use of rules explicit in classroom debriefing of problems and helping students to think algorithmically about the actions that a particular process comprises—to think of the process as an entity that takes input and yields output" (p. 47). I would argue that this type of thinking should be encouraged and developed in primary grades. This type of thinking is a definite extension of how we view the idea of algebra and indicates the rethinking necessary to promote this type of reasoning with all students, regardless of their grade level.

Chapter

9

Using Peer and
Self-Assessment Effectively

Students should be involved in the assessment of their learning. Peer and self-assessment methods give students an active role in understanding their own strengths and weaknesses. NCTM (1995), in its standards document dealing with assessment in mathematics, asserts that assessment that enhances mathematical learning should become a routine part of classroom activity and not an interruption. Regular and student-oriented assessment practices support this goal. As students reflect on their progress and are engaged with the teacher and their peers in assessing their understanding of mathematics, they develop important skills in monitoring their learning. This active and engaged environment is characterized by a climate in which students feel safe to exchange ideas, critique their own and their peers' work, and discuss strengths and weaknesses in mathematical thinking. This type of assessment environment encourages student accountability and promotes rich mathematical understanding. This chapter will focus on how peer and self-assessment of mathematical writing can be used effectively in such an environment.

Peer Review and Assessment

Mathematical communication includes students' analyzing and evaluating the mathematical thinking and strategies of others, one of the goals of the NCTM (2000) communication standard. The process of considering, discussing, evaluating, and reflecting helps students to build knowledge about processes, strategies, methods, and concepts. Students' critical thinking about the work of others also helps them to become critical thinkers about their own mathematical understanding. Writing provides a record of an individual's mathematical thinking and provides students with a substantive springboard for considering the strength and weaknesses of mathematical ideas, concepts, and applications—a powerful milieu in which to develop mathematical understanding.

Students at all grade levels can engage in some type of peer review of their writing, either in pairs or in small groups. Responding to the writing of peers gives students an opportunity to check their thinking and see how others express their mathematical understanding. It reinforces the use of a common language—a growing technical and sophisticated register through which mathematical ideas and concepts are described. Early experiences with peer review must be done carefully so that students develop expectations about the peer review process. Early elementary experiences might focus on emerging word usage, particularly words that carry a great deal of meaning such as *more, less,* or *same.* Research shows that first- and second-grade students can develop such assessment skills (Black & William, 1998). In one study, the mathematics achievement of first-grade students was positively affected as a result of implementing peer-assisted learning strategies (Fuchs, Yazdian, & Powell, 2002). A study with kindergarten students using peer-mediated methods while studying whole-number sense found that such methods improve student learning (Fuchs, Fuchs, & Karns, 2001). Peer-mediated processes involve peer assessment procedures and can be effectively implemented in classrooms at all age levels. This is promising evidence for supporting a writing-to-learn approach in mathematics that includes substantive peer assessment interactions.

As students progress through elementary school, they are able to engage more extensively in review of their peers' writing. By the fourth grade, students are able to respond critically to their own writing as well as others' work (National Assessment Governing Board, 1998). Students engage in revision for specific goals and precise language and sequencing. By the eighth grade, students have a deeper understanding of their own writing processes and can respond to a variety of texts and use writing mechanics that clarify meaning. By the 12th grade, students will be able to identify and manipulate writing so that it enhances and facilitates understanding. These developmental changes will greatly impact how teachers plan for and implement peer assessment opportunities.

Peer review promotes mathematical communication and extends students' understanding of mathematical ideas and concepts. The type of social interaction indicative of peer assessment requires students to externalize their thinking so that it becomes visible and accessible to themselves and others (Tynjala et al., 2001). The interaction also makes it possible to share and develop meaning that is essential to promote mathematical understanding. In addition, peer review that is carefully monitored by the teacher supports communication of expectations and helps students to internalize standards for good mathematical reasoning. Peer assessment is intricately related to student perceptions about grading and assessment practices. These perceptions include the following (Brookhart, 2004):

- What the task or assignment actually means—the goal of the problem or task
- What it means to do good work
- Levels of difficulty and one's beliefs about one's ability to respond to the task or problem
- The importance of a task or an assignment
- Whether the task is worthwhile to learning
- Self-monitoring abilities to assess the quality of one's own work

Although little research exists on the benefits of peer and self-assessments, there is some research focusing on the complex pattern of links among assessment, feedback, and learning. These studies suggest that challenging assignments and extensive feedback lead to a greater engagement of students and, consequently, higher achievement (Black & Williams, 1998).[1] Peer assessment has been shown to positively impact attitudes toward writing (Katstra, Tollefson, & Gilbert, 2001). Both peer and self-assessment require students to understand criteria and apply them while also necessitating reflection and critical thinking.

Self-Review and Assessment

Self-review and peer assessment practices are intrinsically related. Both are related to reflective thinking. Practices that involve self-evaluation and reflection require elaboration or the transformation of knowledge (Linnakyla, 2001). This process involves giving reasons for the decisions that are made and justifying them, reflecting on individual performance, and discussing the significance and success on tasks. Self-reflective behaviors assist students in developing an awareness of their strengths and weaknesses, which is associated with success in mathematics performance (Kenney & Silver, 1993).[2] The types of questions that promote self-reflection are core to the writing framework that has been developed in this work, including having students focus on what they are doing, why they are doing it, and how it helps them to obtain their result or outcome.

The type of self-assessment skills shown to have a positive impact on student performance (McDonald & Boud, 2003) are similar to those being emphasized throughout this book. These self-assessment skills focus on constructing, validating, applying, and evaluating criteria for student products. Students have the opportunity to engage in naming assessment features or criteria and giving reasons for assessing the quality or worth of their work. Self-assessment skills must be developed, so teachers should provide direction and monitor self-assessment practices. As is the case with developing any new classroom procedure, students need feedback and modeling of suitable assessment behaviors. Paris and Paris (2001) contend that periodic self-assessment of both the processes of learning and the outcomes promotes monitoring of progress, stimulates repair (or corrective) strategies, and builds self-efficacy. The impact of student self-assessment on learning indicates that the initial effort and time required to develop the necessary skills for effective implementation are worth the return in terms of student performance and affective outcomes.

Putting Peer and Self-Assessment Into Practice

The implementation of these assessment practices involves developing students' capabilities for self-review and peer assessment. The following guidelines outline the essential elements of establishing effective peer review and self-assessment practices in the classroom.

1. Students should understand what is required of them as assessors.

2. Students should understand the criteria necessary to make sound judgments.

3. Students should have the opportunity to see assessment modeled and to practice assessment of written products.

Students should be provided with modeling by the teacher, who engages the class through discussion about how these processes work. Many rubrics and assessment tools are developed for adult audiences (Kenney & Silver, 1993). Consider the rubric that is used in the classroom to assess students' writing and make any modifications that are necessary so that it is easily accessible to students. Particularly with elementary students, a simplified and concise rubric based on the one used by the teacher might be necessary to fully engage students in the assessment process.

Using Examples From National Assessments

One approach taken by a fourth-grade teacher involved using items from the National Assessment of Educational Progress (NAEP) as artifacts for developing assessment skills. The NAEP assessment items are also available for grades 4, 8, and 12. Some items are common across all three grade levels and can be used at any level from grade 4 through 12. The teacher in this case also used the NAEP rubric for these modeling exercises and for many of the writing tasks given to her students. The released items from the NAEP provide a good source of problems and responses for teachers to use in developing problem-solving and assessment skills.

In the NAEP example (National Center for Education Statistics, 2004) shown in Figure 9-1, students were asked to provide an answer and explanation. As the teacher introduced this item to her class, she asked the students to focus on the correctness of the answer and whether the explanation gave enough detail. The teacher said that using such items was very helpful in developing assessment skills because the sample items were not from students in the class. She thought that this encouraged everyone to participate in identifying weaknesses and making recommendations.

Students worked in small groups to determine the correctness of the answer and discuss the explanation provided in the sample response. This provided students with an opportunity to further develop their understanding of linear relationships, the topic of several lessons over the past week. It also gave students an opportunity to think about how to assess the explanation in the sample.

Students then came back together for a whole-class discussion of the problem and explanation. The discussion focused on the correct answer provided in the sample item and how the explanation didn't

The table below shows how the chirping of a cricket is related to the temperature outside. For example, a cricket chirps 144 times each minute when the temperature is 76°.

Number of Chirps per Minute	Temperature
144	76°
152	78°
160	80°
168	82°
176	84°

What would be the number of chirps per minute when the temperature outside is 90° if this pattern stays the same?

Answer: 200

Explain how you figured out your answer.

I got my anser by contine-ing the graph until I got to 90°F Then I did the same on the other side

If you need more room for your work, use the space below.

Figure 9-1. NAEP Fourth-Grade Item and Student Response

provide enough detail to understand what the student had done. The discussion also focused on how this response could be revised to receive an extended rating. Students' responses focused on providing clear information about the amount of change, a central element emphasized in instruction over the last week. Students agreed that an extended response would include information about how the chirps increase by 8 for every temperature change of 2°.

The teacher then selected another sample response for the test item and modeled thinking through the assessment process based on the sample student response. NAEP provides additional sample responses and a scoring chart (Figure 9-2) that can help the classroom teacher stimulate discussion of the strengths and weakness in the sample responses. Use of the NAEP items facilitates students' experiences with assessment, gives them practice evaluating items, allows them to see other students and the teacher think through assessment processes, and provides a foundation for implementing classroom assessment criteria.

Scoring Guide

Solution:
200
For every 2° that the temperature increases, the number of chirps increases by 8.

Score & Description

Extended

Answers 200 with explanation that indicates number of chirps increases by 8 for every temperature increase of 2°.

Satisfactory

Gives explanation that describes ratio, but does not carry process far enough (e.g., gives correct answer for 86° [184] or 88° [192] or carries process too far [answers 208]).
OR
Answers 200 and shows 184 86°, 192 88°, 200 90° but gives no explanation.
OR
Answers 200 with explanation that is not stated well but conveys the correct ratio.
OR
Gives clear description of ratio and clearly has minor computational error (e.g., adds incorrectly).

Partial

Answers between 176 and 208, inclusive, with explanation that says chirps increase as temperature increases.
OR
Answers between 176 and 208, inclusive, with explanation that they counted by 8 (or by 2).
OR
Uses a correct pattern or process (includes adding a number 3 times or showing 184 and 86 in chart) or demonstrates correct ratio.
OR
Has half the chart with 200 on the answer line.
OR
"I added 24" (with 200 on answer line).

Minimal

Answers between 176 and 208, inclusive, with no explanation or irrelevant or incomplete explanation.
OR
Has explanation that number of chirps increases as temperature increases but number is not in range.
OR
Has number out of range but indicates part of the process (e.g., I counted by 8s)
OR
Explanation—as temperature increases the chirps increase but number is out of range.

Incorrect

Incorrect response.

Figure 9-2. Scoring Guide for NAEP Test Item

Using Peer Assessment

An eighth-grade mathematics teacher in North Carolina connected writing in mathematics with general preparation for the state-mandated writing test. The writing test typically included a prompt dealing with mathematics and extended responses to a problem situation or task. The teacher used the general rubric for mathematics from the 1997–1998 North Carolina Open-Ended Assessment, which would be used to assess students' written responses on the exam. This rubric was used by peers in assessing the quality of writing about mathematical tasks and problems. It rates students' writing as follows:

3: All parts of the question are answered accurately and completely. All directions are followed.

2: Answer deals correctly with most aspects of the question, but something is missing. May deal with all aspects but have minor errors.

1: Addresses item but only partially correct; something correct related to the question.

0: Answer is unresponsive, unrelated, or inappropriate. Nothing is correct.

The teacher applied the following approach in implementing peer assessment as part of writing in mathematics. First, students working independently constructed a written response to a prompt related to a mathematical task or problem. Second, students exchanged their written products with a peer and applied the general rubric to assign a rating. Third, students had to supply a justification for their rating, including suggestions for improving the quality of the writing. Fourth, students revised their writing, maintaining the original product so that both could be viewed by the teacher. Fifth, a whole-class discussion focused on strengths and weaknesses in the written responses of the students (Pugalee, 2001a).

In the following example, students were responding to the following prompt: "If a swimming pool has a perimeter of 18 meters and covers an area of 18 square meters, what are its dimensions?"

The first student response (Figure 9-3) received a 2. This student found the correct answer of 3 meters by 6 meters. His partner, however, gave him a rating of 2, explaining as follows: "You did very well getting the correct answer. You explained how you find the perimeter, but you nearly forgot the area. You need something in the problem about how you found the area."

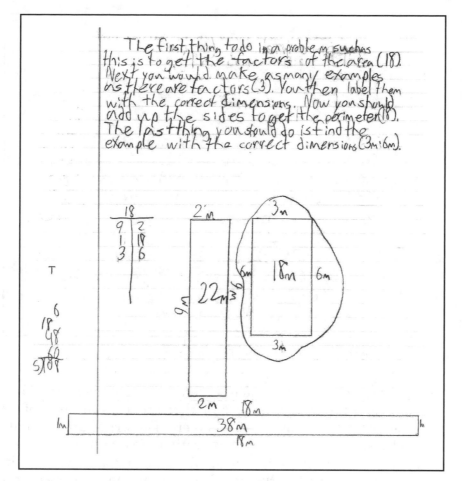

Figure 9-3.   Student Response to Pool Problem With a Rating of 2

The goal of peer assessment is to help students reason mathematically and communicate their thinking effectively. In this example, the evaluator realizes that more detail about an important component of the problem isn't clear, although it can be inferred from the diagrams. This kind of feedback provides the writer with information that makes his or her communication more effective.

In the example shown in Figure 9-4, the student received a 3. The peer rater supplied four reasons for the rating. "First, you have the correct answer of 6 by 3. Second, you show how you found all the possible factors for the area. Third, you do a good job explaining how to find the perimeter and which pair gives you 18. Fourth, you begin by giving your answer and end that way, too. You should write *meters* after your *6* and *3*."

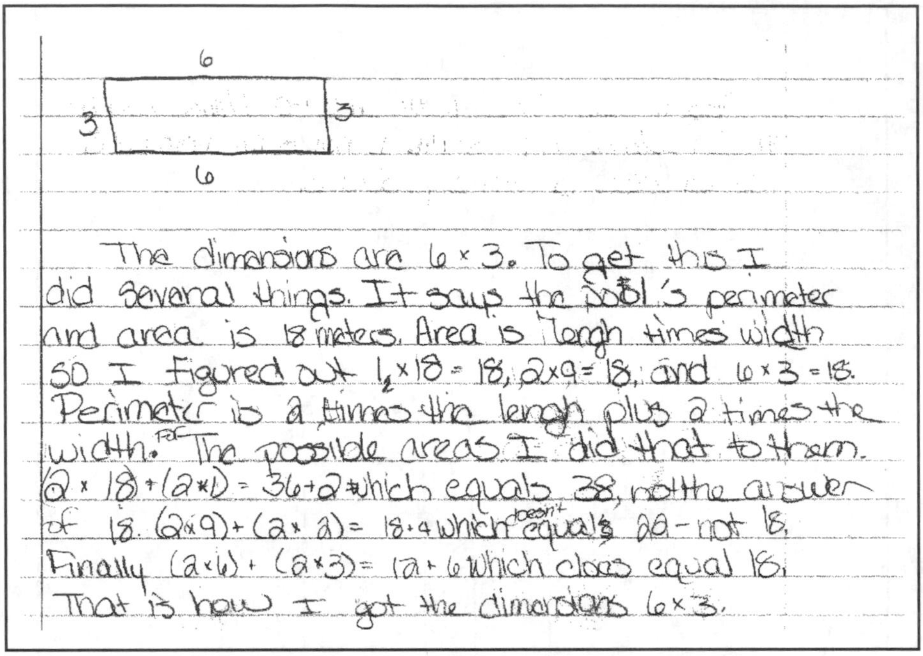

The dimensions are 6 × 3. To get this I
did several things. It says the pool's perimeter
and area is 18 meters. Area is length times width
so I figured out 1 × 18 = 18, 2×9 = 18, and 6 × 3 = 18.
Perimeter is 2 times the length plus 2 times the
width. The possible areas. I did that to them.
(2 × 18) + (2 × 1) = 36 + 2 which equals 38, not the answer
of 18. (2×9) + (2 × 2) = 18 · 4 which doesn't equals 22 - not 18.
Finally (2×6) + (2×3) = 12 + 6 which does equal 18.
That is how I got the dimensions 6 × 3.

Figure 9-4. Student Response to Pool Problem With a Rating of 3

This peer response shows a clear understanding of the mathematical processes to find the number pair that produces an area of 18 square meters and a perimeter of 18 meters. The writer understands clearly why she received the highest rating: a correct answer and clear explanations of finding the combination that would result in the necessary area and perimeter. Notice that the rater also provided a suggestion to add the units (meters) after the dimensions. Specifying units is very important in mathematics as well as in real-world applications. The teacher might decide to follow up with a whole-class discussion on the importance of units if the problem is common. Many mathematics teachers have a policy that an answer without the appropriate units is not complete, so the student would not receive the highest rating.

Using Self-Assessment

Students at all grade levels can develop the self-reflective skills that will empower them to consider their own mathematical thinking. Students will need direction and training in this process, but it will contribute to higher achievement (McDonald & Boud). Regardless of the depth or length of the writing task, students should be given

opportunities to think about their performance. The following paragraphs describe two self-assessment instruments: one for elementary students and one for upper elementary through secondary
students. Both of the instruments focus on problem solving and students' abilities to describe those processes.

The elementary instrument (Figure 9-5) allows students to select
an appropriate icon to show how they feel about their behavior as it
relates to the given statement. The four statements closely follow
the problem-solving heuristic offered by Polya (1957). The first statement asks the students whether they understood the problem. This
is an important initial step that will assist students in becoming
more self-evaluative about their initial understanding of a problem.
Students should be encouraged to identify specifically what made
the problem difficult to understand. In addition to being an effective
self-assessment instrument, this scale provides information that the
teacher can select for follow-up. The second and third items reflect
the importance of developing and carrying out a plan and being able
to describe those components. These items take problem solving to a
level where being able to communicate mathematically is important.
Students' reasoning abilities will become more refined if they are
given frequent oppor-
tunities to think and
describe their math-
ematical plans and
actions. The last item
asks the student if
they checked their
work. It is important
for students to think
about the reasonable-
ness of their solution
and the accuracy of
their work. The item
reflects the students'
confidence in their
work.

The problem-solving
rating scale (Figure 9-
6) has an approach
similar to that followed
in the elementary self-
assessment grid. The
first two items focus

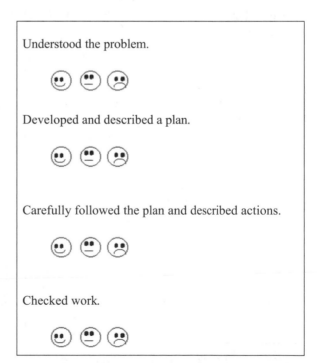

Figure 9-5. Elementary Self-Assessment Check-
list

the students' attention on how well they understood the problem, including recognizing important and unimportant information, and they include another very important feature—being able to explain the problem. This is a very good mechanism through which to build students' abilities to think about a problem and the information essential to solving that problem, and then being able to describe the problem concisely and accurately. The third prompt concerns the students' abilities to implement a plan and describe their thinking. The emphasis here is on being able to give details about actions. Teachers can emphasize and develop expectations that focus on mathematical reasoning and justification. The last statement asks students to reflect on the level of difficulty of the problem. This gives the students an opportunity to think back over their experience with the problem and their ability to effectively solve it.

These checklists can be effectively used along with rubrics for evaluating mathematical writing. The self-assessment checklists give students an opportunity to think about their actions. It is important for students to use the rubrics (or comparable student-friendly versions) that will be used in class when engaging in self-assessment. Consider how two students self-assessed their work using the eighth-grade rubric discussed earlier in this chapter. Students were responding to the following prompt:

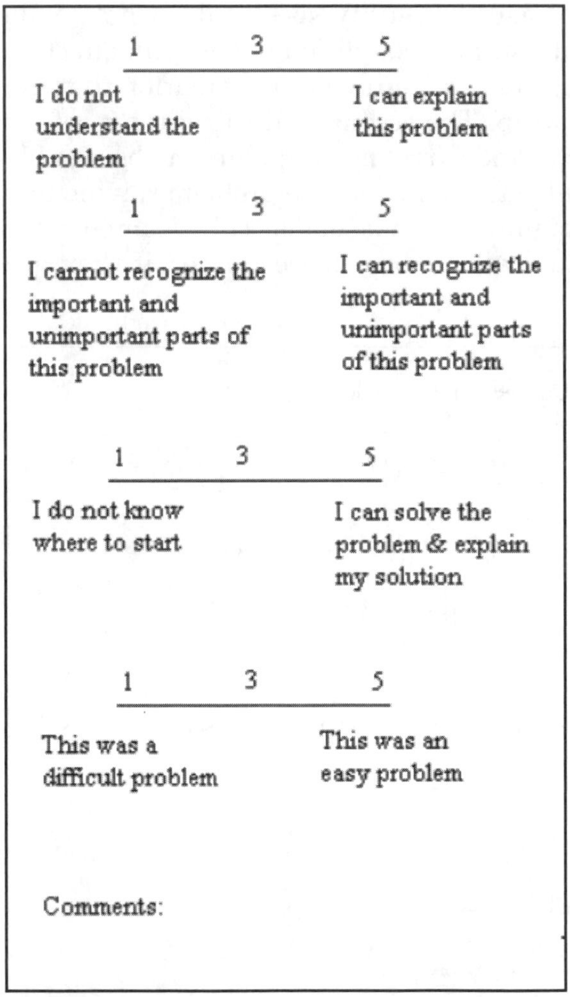

1	3	5
I do not understand the problem		I can explain this problem

1	3	5
I cannot recognize the important and unimportant parts of this problem		I can recognize the important and unimportant parts of this problem

1	3	5
I do not know where to start		I can solve the problem & explain my solution

1	3	5
This was a difficult problem		This was an easy problem

Comments:

Figure 9-6. Problem-Solving Rating Scale
(From *Alaska Department of Education & Early Development*)

"7 + (–10) is equal to –3; but –7 + 10 is equal to 3. Why is one of these answers positive and one negative? Describe why the rule works."

The student producing the response in Figure 9-7 gave herself a rating of 3. She indicated that she answered all parts of the question and provided good reasons that the rule worked. The teacher expected students to tell how they could improve their response. This student stated, "My last sentence could be clearer. I know that absolute value is important. I just can't figure out how to say it."

One of these answers is positive and one of these answers is negative because the absolute value of 10 is higher than the absolute value of seven, so if the negative is with the ten, then the answer is negative, but if it's with the seven than it's positive. You take the sign of the higher absolute value. It works because there is more of the number with the higher absolute value, than that of the one with the lowest.

Figure 9-7. Positive and Negative Sums Problem With a Rating of 3

The student producing the second response (Figure 9-8) gave herself a rating of 2. She indicated that although she wrote a long response, she couldn't really answer the second part of telling why the rule worked. "I know the rule. Wish I could tell why it works." The student's self-reflection shows that she is able to reasonably evaluate her work and identify weaknesses.

When you add integers you must look at the signs of the numbers. If the signs are alike you add them. If you have unlike signs you subtract the numbers and take the sign with the number that has the highest number value. Both problems have different signs. In the 1st problem the 10 is negative, in the 2nd problem the 7 is negative. In the 1st problem you subtract and take the sign from the 10 because it has a bigger value. In the 2nd problem you also subtract and also take the sign from the 10 because it is of bigger value.

Figure 9-8. Positive and Negative Sums Problem With a Rating of 2

These self-assessment procedures work best when they are used to further discussion and development of key ideas and concepts. From these two examples, it is clear that students still have difficulty understanding the rule for adding integers. They have well-developed procedural understanding but lack the comprehension of key concepts that would demonstrate conceptual understanding. The students need more experiences working with the concept of absolute value and developing an understanding of how the distance an integer is from zero impacts the sum of the integers. A follow-up experience might involve additional demonstrations using number lines to model the addition of integers. It is clear from these self-assessments that the reflections provide substantive feedback that can impact the teacher's next instructional steps.

Summary

Peer review and self-assessment can be effective components of a systematic and regular feedback loop that engages students and teachers in analyzing and critiquing the mathematical writing of others. There is a generally high agreement between teachers' assessments and peer reviews or self-assessments (Black & William, 1998). First- and second-grade students' self-assessment ratings agree with teachers' ratings the majority of the time, with differences typically being instances where teachers rated students higher than students rated themselves (Higgins, Harris, & Kuehn, 1994). Peer reviews and self-assessments align with teacher expectations for learning goals and contribute positively to students' perceptions of their ability to perform well and their learning or achievement.

Notes

1. Black and Williams' (1998) review of research on formative assessment indicates that innovative practices characterized by frequent feedback about learning results in substantial learning gains. Their review includes a theoretical discussion outlining the development of models for formative assessment and the prospects for improving practice. Regular feedback systems also positively impact students' beliefs about their own capacity as learners, which can affect achievement. Some research suggests that self-evaluation practices, if combined with performance goals, improve persistence, self-efficacy, and achievement. This important review of research supports a writing-to-learn mathematics program that has assessment as a core component. Peer and self-assessment provide the regular and frequent feedback systems that, along with performance goals, are characteristic of assessment systems that produce gains in student learning.

2. Kenney and Silver (1993) summarize key findings from the literature on mathematical problem solving. Individuals who are successful with mathematical problem-solving tasks are characterized as having a collection of strategies available to them but also have skills to reflect on the problem-solving activities effectively and efficiently. Students who are less successful do not function as well in self-reflective or self-evaluative situations. From these studies, it appears that self-assessment practices that are carefully monitored and designed by teachers should assist students in developing reflective skills that are related to successful problem solving. The emphasis on writing and assessment throughout this book has included the importance of students reflecting on their strategies and approaches, thus providing students with multiple approaches to consider and evaluate.

Following Up

Extending Students' Mathematical Understanding

As writing in mathematics becomes an integral part of the instructional landscape of the classroom, students will become better at communicating mathematical ideas. They will become more sophisticated in their mathematical writing, and their writing and doing of mathematics will support the development of metacognitive thinking. The primary goal of writing programs in mathematics is to develop students' abilities to understand concepts and ideas in meaningful and rich ways. As students become familiar with the process of writing-to-learn in mathematics, teachers can focus on using writing to extend students' thinking and reasoning. This chapter will focus on those next steps and provide some thinking points about extending students' mathematical writing skills and consequently their thinking and reasoning skills.

Becoming Better Mathematical Writers

As students write more and reflect on their thinking, they will extend their abilities to communicate their solutions and thinking processes related to mathematical tasks and problems. Students will become more competent to clearly and concisely organize, structure, reason, and describe important mathematical concepts and ideas. They will become mathematical thinkers, and that thinking will become visible through their writing. The teacher's goal throughout this process of writing in mathematics is to extend students' mathematical understanding.

Writing templates or models can provide students with the structure that will help them to extend their thinking about mathematical ideas, concepts, and processes. Such models are intricately related to developing metacognitive skills, which will be discussed in detail later in this chapter. The proposed model (Table 10-1) consists of three phases that contain several questions to guide students' thinking. The model, Review-Respond-Reflect,[1] is intended as a mechanism to support students mathematical reasoning and reflection on their own learning.

Table 10-1.   Review-Respond-Reflect Model

Review
What are the big mathematical ideas in the problem or task?
What do I know about these concepts, ideas, procedures, theorems, and definitions? How do they relate to the task?
Respond
What plan or process is necessary to arrive at a solution or an outcome?
Why am I making those decisions or claims?
Reflect
Is my outcome reasonable? Why?
How have my ideas and knowledge changed?

Review requires students to identify the key ideas and information in the task. This includes understanding the problem situation or task and identifying related key concepts and ideas. As students identify these important pieces of information, they are asked to think about what they currently know about the topic. This provides students with an opportunity to identify what they know, and it also provides an initial evaluation of the adequacy of that level of knowledge or understanding.

Respond requires students to develop a plan or action. Students identify the procedures or processes that are necessary to respond to the task. It is important for students to become accustomed to relating steps or actions to the mathematics that support them. Through these considerations, students' mathematical reasoning skills are reinforced. The aim is to develop thinkers who are reflective and customarily justify and reason about the mathematics that supports their actions.

Reflect engages students in revisiting their work and thinking about their solution or outcome. Having students focus on why their outcome is reasonable is recursive in that it brings them again to the mathematics that supports their actions. Students should be encouraged to think about how their ideas and knowledge changed as they reflected and wrote about the task or problem. This action cycles back to the initial Review phase as students think once again about what they knew and how that knowledge was applied and changed.

Extending students' writing provides outstanding possibilities to improve the critical and creative thinking skills of students. Critical thinking may be viewed as thinking that involves examining, relating, and evaluating the multiple features of a problem or task. Creative thinking is thinking that is original and reflective, producing a complex product characterized by a synthesis of ideas, a generation of new ideas, and an evaluation of their effectiveness (Krulik & Rudnick, 1999). This level of thinking extends typical heuristics by extending reflection on the task characterized by the following questions (p. 139): What's another way? What if . . . ? What's wrong? What would you do?

Focused writing in mathematics reinforces the type of thinking that is characteristic of creative and critical thinking. Consider the following example, which illustrates how mathematical reasoning can be extended and nurtured through students' mathematical writing. In this example (Figure 10-1) eighth-grade students were given four rectangles and asked to investigate the relationships between them. When the students, working in small groups, had discovered that some of the rectangles were similar, the teacher asked the students to align the rectangles so that they shared a common vertex and to pay particular attention to the diagonals of the rectangles. Students were instructed to work together but then write individual descriptions of the relationship, including a mathematical justification for that relationship.

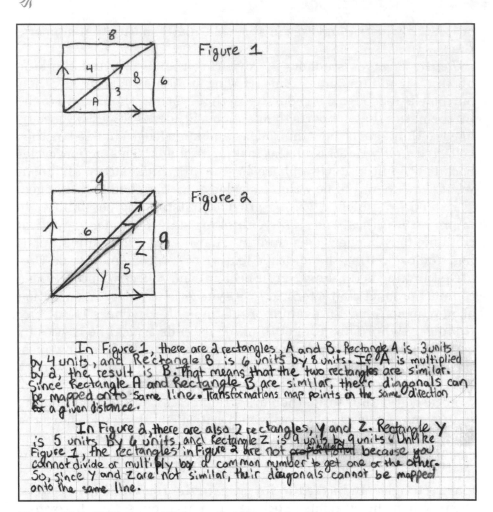

In Figure 1, there are 2 rectangles, A and B. Rectangle A is 3 units by 4 units, and Rectangle B is 6 units by 8 units. If A is multiplied by 2, the result is B. That means that the two rectangles are similar. Since Rectangle A and Rectangle B are similar, their diagonals can be mapped onto same line. Transformations map points on the same direction for a given distance.

In Figure 2, there are also 2 rectangles, Y and Z. Rectangle Y is 5 units by 6 units, and Rectangle Z is 9 units by 9 units. Unlike Figure 1, the rectangles in Figure 2 are not proportional because you cannot divide or multiply by a common number to get one or the other. So, since Y and Z are not similar, their diagonals cannot be mapped onto the same line.

Figure 10-1. Writing and Mathematical Reasoning Task

In this example, mathematical reasoning is evident. The student explains that two of the rectangles are similar and justifies that conclusion by noting that the dimensions of one rectangle are found by multiplying the dimensions of the smaller one by 2. The student continues to explain that the diagonals of these similar rectangles are on the same line. The student uses the idea of transformations and mapping to argue that the points are mapped in the same direction for a given distance. The student revisits the idea of a scale factor when discussing why the two nonsimilar rectangles do not have diagonals on the same line. Other students in this class drew the rectangles in the Cartesian plane and used the coordinates to show that the diagonals of similar rectangles, when aligned at a common vertex, would have the same equation for the diagonal line.

Mathematical reasoning, as demonstrated in this response, should be an outcome of a strong mathematics program. This level of thinking shows how writing can support the development of mathematical reasoning skills.

The next example (Figure 10-2), from a secondary school course in advanced mathematics, further demonstrates the connection between mathematical reasoning and writing. Students were routinely given

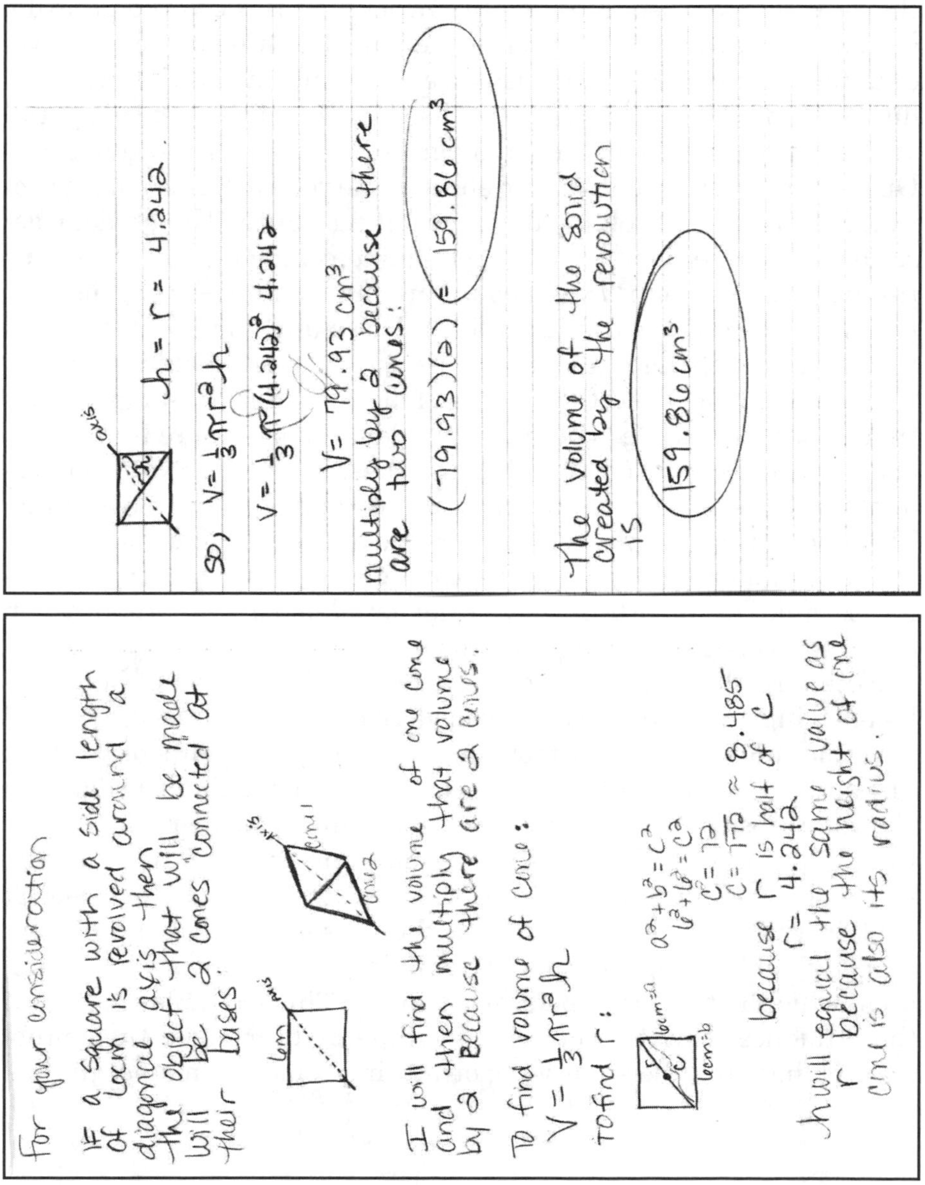

Figure 10-2. Advanced Mathematics Example

a problem that they worked on during the week and one for which they were to write a description detailing how they solved it. The following task was given in the first semester of the course: "A square with a side of length 6 cm is revolved about a diagonal as an axis. Find the volume of the solid created by the revolution." The teacher's goal was to get students involved in thinking about their problem-solving approaches and to describe them.

As students write about their thinking, it becomes clear whether they are able to reason through the various steps they take toward a solution to a task or problem. This student clearly describes his level of understanding. First, he visualizes how such a rotation will produce "2 cones 'connected' at their bases." The student's keen spatial visualization is evident in the diagrams as well as the narrative. Once the student visualizes the effect of the rotation, it is a matter of thinking about the volume of the resulting figure. The student describes his process step by step, providing comments as he reasons through the problem. "H will equal the same value as r because the height of one cone is also its radius." These and similar statements reveal how he thought about why his actions were making sense.

These examples and the one that follows (Figure 10-3) exemplify that as students write about their problem solving, there is a heightened awareness of their thinking and reasoning. Often younger students will use diagrams or pictures to represent their thinking. Through writing, they can be encouraged to describe and justify their thinking. Figure 10-3 is from a second grader. This student's drawing became an important part of her problem-solving organization and a tool for reflecting on the problem.

Note how the diagram and the student's description of her problem-solving processes are intertwined. She drew pictures and labeled the time (minutes) that it took for the various segments of the trip. She added the numbers and came up with 75. Note that the diagram shows that she realized that the return walk from the park to home was 30 minutes. Then she shows some remarkable reflection. She subtracts 60 minutes from 75 to get 15 minutes. Although she doesn't explain this fully, she is verifying the reasonableness of her solution. By subtracting the time for walking, she is left with 15 minutes, which is the time spent at the park. This example illustrates the influence of writing on helping students to monitor their problem-solving processes—very important in promoting metacognition.

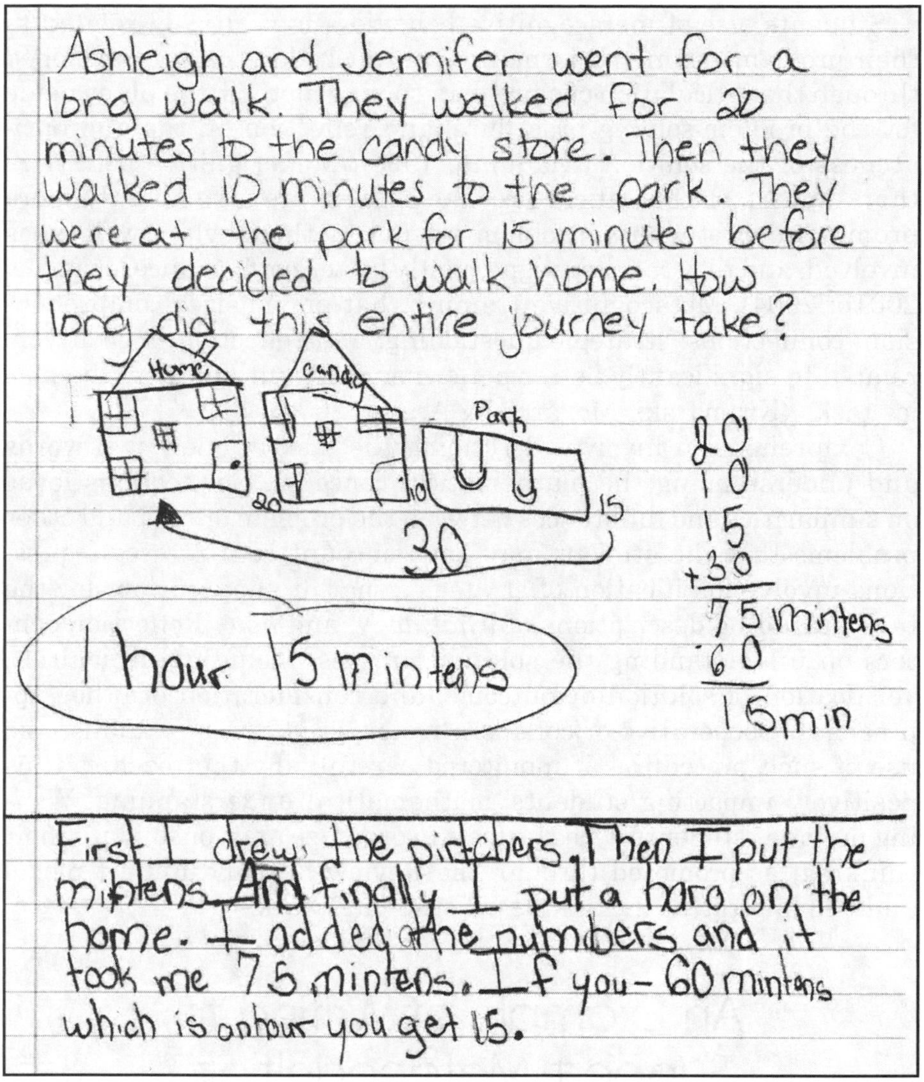

Figure 10-3. Second Grader's Problem Solving

Promoting Metacognition

Metacognition includes knowledge of resources and control of thinking. In general, metacognition may be thought of as thinking about thinking. Writing-to-learn interventions that engage students in reflecting on their current knowledge, their confusions, and their learning processes are particularly effective in providing scaffolding that promotes metacognitive processes (Bangert-Drowns, Hurley, & Wilkinson, 2004).

Students' use of metacognitive behaviors is positively related to their problem-solving performance, and such skills can be developed through the articulation of a problem-solving method, the plans made for the problem-solving procedure, and reflection on the appropriateness of the solution (Oladunni, 1998). Metacognitive behaviors that support mathematical problem solving are significantly more prominent in students' problem-solving methods when writing is involved, and they result in significantly better performance (Pugalee, 2001b; 2004). Metacognitive training that emphasizes comprehension, connections, strategic questioning, and reflection is positively related to significantly better performance on authentic mathematics tasks (Kramarski, Mevarch, & Arami, 2002).

Comprehension involves describing the task in one's own words and understanding the mathematical concepts. Connections focus on similarities and differences between the problem or task and other problems that the student may have encountered. Strategic questions involve justification of strategies that are appropriate for the task, including descriptions of *what, why,* and *how.* Reflection centers on understanding the solution process, including difficulties, verification of solution or outcome, and consideration of other approaches. Cooperative or collaborative experiences can enhance the use of such procedures if monitored carefully by the teacher, thus positively impacting students' mathematical understanding. Writing provides students with the tools to organize and consolidate their thinking, as promoted through the Review-Respond-Reflect model and demonstrated in examples of students' work.

An Example of Writing to Support Metacognition

The previous examples show how writing provides a reflective tool that helps students to monitor and reason about their thinking, thus developing metacognitive skills. Writing exercises can be explicitly structured to support students in reflecting on the content or task. The following writing sample (Figure 10-4) shows the approach of a sixth-grade teacher in promoting reflective thinking. The format is a derivation of the K-W-L strategy, a popular reading comprehension strategy. K stands for what is already known, W for what one wants to learn about the topic, and L for what was learned. This teacher replaces the W with "what I still need to know about the topic."

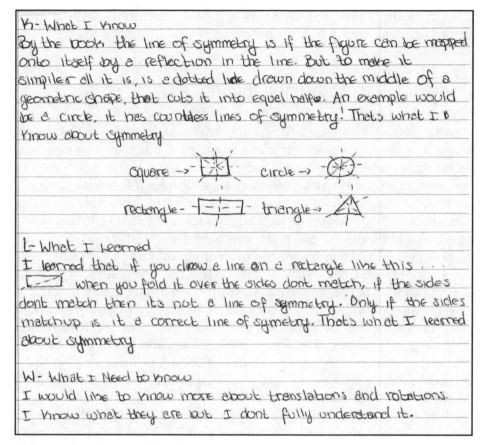

K - What I know

By the book the line of symmetry is if the figure can be mapped onto itself by a reflection in the line. But to make it simpler all it is, is a dotted line drawn down the middle of a geometric shape, that cuts it into equal halfs. An example would be a circle, it has countless lines of symmetry! Thats what I know about symmetry

square → ☒   circle → ⊛

rectangle - ⊟ - triangle → △

L - What I Learned

I learned that if you draw a line on a rectangle like this . . . ▭ when you fold it over the sides dont match, if the sides dont match then it's not a line of symmetry. Only if the sides match up is it a correct line of symmetry. Thats what I learned about symmetry

W - What I Need to know

I would like to know more about translations and rotations. I know what they are but I dont fully understand it.

Figure 10-4. A Modified K-W-L

Although this particular example is used as a reading strategy, it provides the structure and support to assist students in approaching mathematical tasks or problems. The students write what they know about symmetry, but they use the text to give this knowledge a foundation. As the students reflect on what they learned, there is a discussion of how to determine if a figure has symmetry. It is clear how this student's new information about symmetry relates to what is already known. As a result of considering the information, the student wants to know more about translations and rotations.

It is important for students to realize what information would help them to better understand a topic or concept. This writing structure provides a frame in which students can reflect on their current understanding and construct new knowledge. This particular framework could be further modified to support metacognitive thinking. For example, the strategy could use the following questions: What do I know about the mathematics related to the problem? What did

I learn or apply in completing this task? What related mathematical topics or ideas would help in better understanding the topic?

Composing Word Problems

Another effective task is to engage students in writing their own story problems. Such experiences frequently build on the personal experiences and interests of students and are a meaningful part of writing activities at the elementary level designed to assist students in the development of formal language arts skills (Martinez & Martinez, 2000; Winograd, 1992). Research indicates that this strategy helps students to grasp the mathematical and linguistic structure of problems. In order for the problem to make sense, the student must understand the concept underlying the problem. Using writing assignments emphasizing word-problem types develops an understanding of problem structure and is positively related to student performance on mathematical problem-solving tasks (Rudnitsky, Etheredge, Freeman, & Gilbert, 1995). In addition, teachers can extend the problem-solving knowledge of students by engaging them in the analysis and correction of a particular error or misunderstanding of a mathematical concept or idea.

Winograd (1992), reporting on fifth-graders' construction of math word problems, relates that students' problems are frequently more interesting and challenging than textbook problems. Students also described a good math student as someone who wrote interesting and challenging problems and then worked to understand and solve those problems. Such comments indicate how students internalize views about what it means to be good at mathematics. The following problem, composed by a student, illustrates the points raised in Winograd's research:

Hootie's Money

Hootie is hiring me to count her money. I already counted 15.00 dollars. 5 seconds later I counter 10.00 more dollars. Hootie offered me 2.00 for the job or 10% of the money I counted. Which choice has more money?

The following problem (Figure 10-5) illustrates how elementary students can effectively write problems that reflect mathematical concepts and ideas. Teachers who use this strategy have students exchange problems and solve them or allow students to work in small groups or pairs on collections of student-generated word problems.

This example shows how a second-grade student understands working with fractions. Notice the real-world context for the problem. The student's problem shows that she understands the necessary operations to make the multiple comparisons to solve the problem. From the problem that this student wrote and her solution, it is clear that she understands part-whole relationships and the subtraction of fractions. Being able to write a problem and describe the solution is a positive way for students to connect mathematics concepts, computations, and events in their own lives. The student's diagrams illustrate how she was thinking about the problem situation, the use of fractions in context, and her reasoning about how to solve the problem.

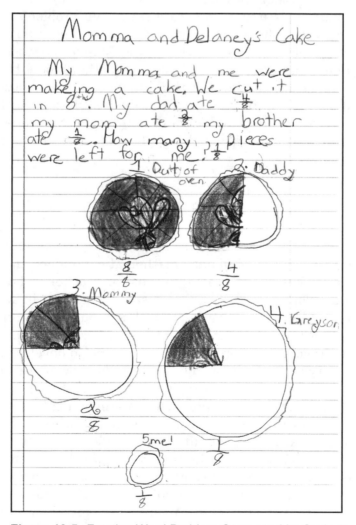

Figure 10-5. Fraction Word Problem Composed by Student

A good follow-up to problems that primarily involve computation and procedures is to have students write a word problem for the task. This gives students an opportunity to apply mathematical skills to problems, develops and reinforces the use of a variety of strategies for mathematical problem solving, and requires students to interpret and understand various contexts for mathematics word problems. For example, an introductory algebra class was working with two-step equations. The teacher asked the students to write a problem that would show $2x + 3 = 45$. One student wrote, "Leone needs 45 dollars to pay a bill but he only has 3 dollars. He can work after school two evenings. How much does he need to make each day?" Another student shared her problem: "Yan has 3 more CDs than David. Together they have 45 CDs. How many CDs does Yan have? David?" As students generate their own problems, they are showing facility with the underlying concepts. These two examples show how students understand the relationship of the various parts of the equation and can construct situations that model those relationships. Consider the level of thinking necessary for students to successfully write problems that fit a given situation. Such activities reinforce conceptual understanding by providing students with an opportunity to think about the application of mathematical concepts and ideas.

Summary

The goal of this chapter was to present some stepping stones for using writing to extend students' mathematical understanding. The strategies presented are considerations for teachers who want to continue developing writing as an instructional tool in ways that further expand students' mathematical communication and mathematical understanding. As students continue developing writing skills in mathematics, more focus can be given to developing mathematical reasoning and metacognitive skills. Review-Respond-Reflect was presented as one framework to more strategically focus students' thinking as they approach a mathematical task or problem. Examples of student writing show how reasoning and metacognitive skills become outcomes of effective writing-to-learn mathematics programs. Student-authored word problems is presented as another promising strategy that helps students to understand the relationship between problems or tasks and the contexts or situations that model them. As students work in writing their own problems, they demonstrate an understanding of the problem structure and the related mathematical concepts and processes. Extending students' mathematical understanding is an ongoing goal of writing in mathematics. Mathematical communication and mathematical understanding develop hand in hand as teachers engage students in writing that focuses on reasoning and metacognition.

Notes

1. The Review-Respond-Reflect model is similar to many models that are used to support writing-to-learn. For example, the Science Writing Heuristic (Hand, Prain & Yore, 2001, p. 118) includes a set of questions corresponding to the 3R model: What are my questions? What did I do? What did I see? What can I claim? How do I know? Why am I making these claims? How do my ideas compare with other ideas? and How have my ideas changed? Similarly, understanding the problem, analyzing the problem, planning, exploring, implementing, and verifying are components of a framework for describing the problem-solving behaviors of students engaged in sense-making (Curcio & Artzt, 1998).

Developing Professional Networks and Supports

This chapter will focus on resources and other supports. Part of the professional environment of teaching includes formulating connections with teachers and other professionals. Also included in this professional landscape is participation in the larger professional community, which includes various interests and organizations beyond the individual school. The wide range of materials and resources available also commands some familiarity. Discussion of these resources and supports is rooted in the goal of building connections at the individual school level and beyond so that the writing and mathematics connection is promoted. Writing in mathematics is not familiar territory for many teachers. This professional landscape requires teachers who are willing to share their valuable expertise and talent. Supports and resources are necessary to provide the framework and information that encourages success.

Building Connections at the School Level

Griffiths and Clyne (1994) offer some ideas that can promote the language and mathematics connection. These ideas include showing products and outcomes to colleagues to get them involved in using writing as a learning tool; collecting resources and references that support writing in mathematics; presenting results to parents at school meetings or information events; presenting results at staff meetings; and suggesting readings for teachers and parents interested in issues related to writing in mathematics.

Build Connections With Other Teachers

Work with teachers at the same grade level or those who teach different subjects to get ideas for writing in mathematics. Teachers can provide information about writing, possible activities or tasks, assessment practices, and other issues. Elementary teachers can follow up with writing activities from mathematics as part of other lessons or work with teachers in other subject areas, such as art or physical education. Middle and secondary teachers can look for topic connections across subjects and work with subject area teachers to develop activities or tasks that support learning goals from multiple content areas. Such collegial relationships can become links in supporting efforts for writing in mathematics by providing information for tasks or problems so that others can follow up on a key concept, skill, or process. Building teacher-to-teacher relationships is imperative for creating structures that support integration of math concepts in appropriate lessons across various disciplines.

The addition of an essay component to the Scholastic Aptitude Test (SAT) provides secondary mathematics teachers with a specific context for extending working relationships with other teachers, particularly those in the language arts. The highest score on the SAT essay, using a holistic rubric, is 6. This score indicates "clear and consistent mastery, although [the essay] may have a few minor errors." This type of essay has the following characteristics (College Board, 2004):

- Effectively and insightfully develops a point of view on the issue and demonstrates outstanding critical thinking, using clearly appropriate examples, reasons, and other evidence to support its position

- Is well organized and clearly focused, demonstrating clear coherence and a smooth progression of ideas

- Exhibits skillful use of language, using a varied, accurate, and apt vocabulary

- Demonstrates meaningful variety in sentence structure

- Is free of most errors in grammar, usage, and mechanics

Notice how these characteristics align with the qualities of writing in mathematics that have been advocated throughout this book. Students who write in mathematics will have additional content applications that build strong communication skills like those assessed in the SAT. Mathematics teachers who develop strong writing in mathematics programs should become leaders in promoting the importance of writing in mathematics and assist other teachers in promoting and setting up programs that emphasize good mathematical writing.

The following example (Figure 11-1) shows how powerful connections and discussions with colleagues can be in supporting the writing

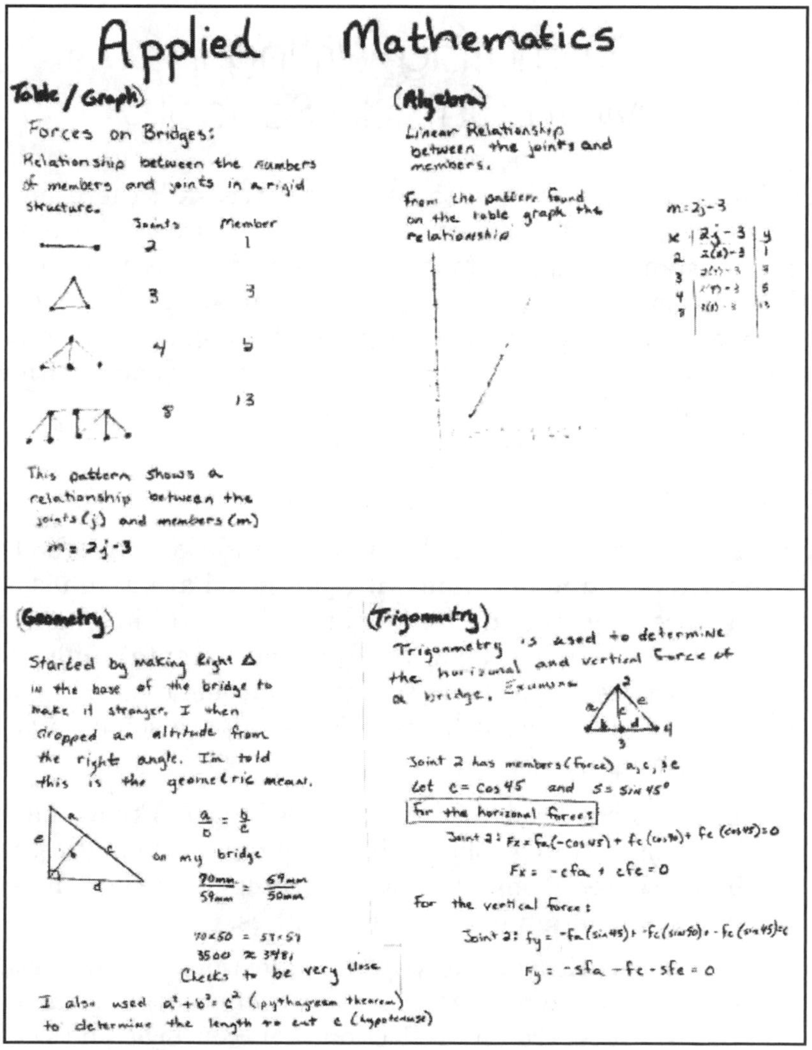

Figure 11-1. Middle School Student's Applied Mathematics Science Project

in mathematics program. The example comes from a middle-grade science teacher who worked with students in extending their mathematical understanding and communication through science projects. This student is exploring the mathematical concepts related to bridges. The segments illustrate the student's reasoning about the number of joints and the importance of right-triangle structures to a bridge's strength. The project demonstrates how writing and reasoning work together in presenting a compelling project. Teachers who expand students' opportunities to explore mathematics and writing in other subjects help students to make important content connections and develop important thinking and reasoning skills.

Promoting Writing in Math Outside School

If writing in mathematics is to be truly successful, there must be broad-based support for efforts outside the classroom. Parents can provide substantial support for writing in mathematics by reinforcing the importance at home and by voicing support at the school and community level. Students can also become engaged in activities outside school that will use and extend their experiences with writing and learning mathematics.

Parents

Any curricular practices that differ from traditional methods are likely to require communication with parents. Parents must know the importance of writing in mathematics. Parental involvement is directly related to student achievement, and parental understanding of key processes employed in teaching mathematics is important for support and follow-up at home.[1] Following are some guidelines for working with parents:

1. Be proactive. From the beginning, let parents know that writing is one strategy that will be used in mathematics. It can be presented along with other strategies that promote students' understanding of mathematics.

2. Be honest. Respond to parents' questions and concerns. If you don't have an immediate answer, let them know that you will research and reflect on their concerns and get back to them.

3. Define accountability. Let parents know how success in writing tasks will be measured.

4. Remember that the bottom line is the benefit of writing in mathematics.

5. Use visual aids and other resources. Present ideas clearly and concisely.

6. Do some examples with parents. This helps parents understand the power of being able to describe mathematical thinking.

7. Keep parents involved. Newsletters can provide descriptions of the mathematics that students are learning and how writing is being used to support that learning. Send key activities home so that parents can work with their children in completing a writing task. Family math nights can provide a way to organize support for your project and to help parents understand how writing and mathematics are related.

Writing and Mathematics Outside the Classroom

A powerful example of students' engagement with mathematics through writing can be found in various online mathematics programs, which provide assistance to students looking for answers to specific questions as well as opportunities to answer challenges and participate in mathematical problem solving. Perhaps one of the better known of these programs is the Math Forum at Drexel University. Its site (www.mathforum.com) provides links to resources and problems for elementary, middle and high school students. In addition, there are resources in Spanish, French, and German for non-native English speakers. The problem of the week provides students with opportunities to write descriptions of their solutions to intriguing problems.

Figure 11-2 demonstrates how writing and mathematics are linked in such mediums. This is an excellent way for students to extend their mathematical thinking and develop their mathematical communication skills. In this example, elementary students used data from 13-year and 17-year cicada cycles to predict when the next 3-year cycle containing no broods of cicadas will occur.

Teachers can also become involved in such projects as mentors who volunteer to encourage students in the various aspects of problem solving and communication. In addition, teachers might involve

From: **Mac Paige**, age 9
School: Deerfield Valley Elementary School, Wilmington, VT

My solution for "Cicada Circus" is that the next 3-year brood gap
is from 2043 to 2045. My solution for the "extra" is that the
17-year brood VIII and the 13-brood XXIII will next come out
together in 2223.
I needed to find out in what year will the next 3-year brood gap of
cicadas will occur. First I added 17 years to all of the original
17-year brood years because that would give me the next
17-year brood years. Next I added 13 years to all of the original
13-year brood years because that would bive me the next
13-year brood years. After that I kept adding to the brood years
because I still didn't have a 3-year gap. Finally I looked at the
numbers and found a 3-year gap between the last part of the 4th
ccle [sic] of 17-year broods and the top of the 5th cycle of 17-year
broods (see the table). My solution for this part of the problem is
that the next 3-year brood gap is from 2043 and [sic] 2045.

I have a prediction. My prediction is that every 51 years there will
be a 3-year gap of no cicadas coming out. I got 51 years by
subtracting 1993 from 2043. I added 51 years to 2042 and 2046
and that equaled 2093 and 2096 (the next 3-year gap). I would
really like it if there were cicadas in Vermont, then we would see
different creatures.

I also needed to find out what year the 17-year brood VIII and the
13-year brood XXIII will meet again. First I found the LCM of 17
and 13 because those are the time periods the cicadas come
out of the ground.

$$17 \times 13 = 221$$

I multiplied 17 and 13 because they're both prime numbers and
prime numbers only have to be muliplied [sic] together to find the
LCM.

Finally I added 221 and 2002 because 2002 is the year the
cicadas came out together.

$$2002 + 221 = 2223$$

That will be 219 years from now!

Figure 11-2. Student Solution Submitted to the Math Forum at Drexel

*(Reproduced with permission from Drexel University (2004) the
Math Forum at Drexel, www.mathforum.com.)*

students on a regular basis in submitting responses to problems.
Teachers can also encourage parents to become involved, either directly
as mentors or indirectly by supporting their child's participation.

E-Mail

E-mail can be an effective way to promote writing outside the classroom. Kramarski & Ritkof (2002) found that e-mail communication
between the teacher and ninth-grade students was effective in learning graphing when the process included an emphasis on metacognitive
thinking (see discussion in chapter 10), which included students

writing explanations to justify their mathematical ideas. The students were able to explain their mathematical reasoning and demonstrated reduced misconceptions about graphs. This electronic community was effective in providing students a forum for expressing their mathematical ideas fluently and flexibly, with explanations including mathematical arguments and rationales in addition to procedural descriptions and summaries. Teachers can explore establishing e-mail mathematics exchanges between students at different schools, between students in different grade levels, such as high school students working with an elementary classroom. Students who are part of teacher education programs would benefit from experiences mentoring students in mathematical problem solving through e-mail exchanges.

Professional Networks and Resources

Look for opportunities to attend professional development offerings that support your ideas. Consider attending mathematics and language arts conferences that offer sessions on writing, language, and mathematics. Consider presenting at a conference. Many states have local chapters of national organizations that provide excellent opportunities for teachers and professionals to share ideas and practices. The national organizations focusing on mathematics and language arts are the National Council of Teachers of Mathematics (NCTM) and the National Council of Teachers of English (NCTE). The International Reading Association (IRA) also provides opportunities for professional involvement that may be of interest to teachers of mathematics. A simple Internet search of the names of these organizations will provide links to their home pages.

In addition to professional organizations, there are numerous listservs and discussion groups to benefit teachers. An Internet search for discussion groups for mathematics teachers yields many possibilities. If there aren't postings related to mathematics and writing, consider starting a discussion. Post a question or share information about your experiences. The Internet provides multiple opportunities for you to connect with professionals from around the world. The connections can be a source of useful ideas and suggestions that support the goal of extending writing as a learning tool for mathematics.

The national professional organizations (NCTM, NCTE, and IRA) provide many resources to guide and support teachers' instruction, as do comparable organizations in England and Australia. The Web sites of these organizations provide multiple resource offerings such as lesson plans and activities, conference and event listings, links to other services, and various publications and products. These sites can be instrumental in searching for resources that support writing in mathematics. The sites allow focused searches that will provide writing in mathematics-related information. In addition, many state departments of education offer Internet-based resources and information.

Lesson plans are readily available at many Internet sites. In addition to searching for lessons, become a contributor of lessons that focus on writing in mathematics. Your experiences and expertise can provide others with the details necessary to successfully use writing as an integral part of mathematics. Check with your state education department to see what types of lesson resources are available and consider submitting your lessons to their database.

Several sites that have a reputation for high-quality resources are worth mentioning, although there are many others. MarcoPolo is a nonprofit consortium that includes national and international educational organizations. The materials are standards-based and include lesson plans, student interactive content, activity sheets, links to panel-reviewed Web sites, and other related resources.

TeacherSource from PBS offers online professional development and a searchable database of lesson plans and activities, including free online videos of teachers modeling math lessons. DiscoverySchool.com offers lesson plans, resources, and educational programming information. The Gateway to Educational Materials (GEM) is sponsored by the U.S. Department of Education and includes a searchable database of lesson plans, activities, and projects.

In addition, the U.S. Department of Education maintains the Educational Resources Information Center (ERIC), which provides a searchable database providing abstracts of educational documents and journals. This is a comprehensive site enabling searches for documents and journal articles. NCTM offers several journals for classroom teachers: *Teaching Children Mathematics, Mathematics Teaching in the Middle School,* and *Mathematics Teacher.* These publications provide classroom-tested ideas, activities, and resource information. In addition to providing substantive reading on important topics for mathematics teaching and learning, these publications are an exceptional outlet for teachers to share their ideas. These journals encourage classroom teachers to submit articles for consideration.

Summary

Writing-to-learn mathematics needs teacher leaders who are willing to share strategies and successes. This chapter highlighted some key strategies that extend the teachers' realm of influence beyond his or her classroom. Building connections with other teachers is essential in forming networks in which collaboration and lesson sharing are the norm. Such relationships ultimately support student learning.

Related to classroom success is parental involvement. A writing-to-learn program needs parents who will be advocates of such an important instructional tool. Opportunities for students to extend their writing outside the classroom include the use of e-mail and participation in online forums that focus on problem solving and mathematical communication.

There are many outlets from which teachers can obtain information to assist in this journey. In addition to professional organizations, there are numerous collections of lessons, activities, documents, articles, and projects. Teachers are encouraged when possible to become contributors to these excellent resource collections. As teachers experience success in planning, implementing, and assessing writing that supports students' development of mathematical literacy, the story must be shared. It is the telling of this story—the sharing of ideas and information—that can dramatically influence the success of writing as an integral part of mathematics teaching and learning.

Note

1. Research indicates that if parents talk to their children about school, express high expectations, and make sure that out-of-school activities are constructive, then the children do better in school. In general, research shows that when families are engaged in their child's education, then the child is more likely to earn higher grades and test scores and enroll in higher level academic programs; be promoted, pass their classes, and earn credits; attend school regularly; have better social skills, improve behavior, and adapt well to school; and go on to postsecondary education (Henderson & Mapp, 2002).

References

Adey, P., Robertson, A., & Venville, G. (2002). Effects of a cognitive acceleration programme on year 1 pupils. *British Journal of Educational Psychology, 72,* 1–25.

Applebee, A., Langer, J., Nystrand, M., & Gamoran, A. (2003). Discussion-based approaches to developing understanding: Classroom instruction in middle and high school English. *American Educational Research Journal, 40* (3), 685–730.

Artz, A. F., & Armour-Thomas, E. (1992). Development of a cognitive-metacognitive framework for protocol analysis of mathematical problem solving in small groups. *Cognition and Instruction, 9* (2), 137–175.

Bangert-Drowns, R. L., Hurley, M. M., & Wilkinson, B. (2004). The effects of school-based writing-to-learn interventions on academic achievement: A meta-analysis. *Review of Educational Research, 74* (1), 29–58.

Black, P., & William, D. (1998). Assessment and classroom learning. *Assessment in Education: Principles, Policy & Practice, 1* (7), 7–74.

Blunk, M. L. (1998). Teacher talk about how to talk in small groups. In M. Lampert & M. L. Blunk (Eds.), *Talking mathematics in school* (pp. 190–212). Cambridge, UK: Cambridge University Press.

Borasi, R., & Siegel, M. (2000). Reading *counts: Expanding the role of reading in mathematics classrooms.* New York: Teachers College Press.

Boscolo, P., & Mason, L. (2001). Writing to learn, writing to transfer. In P. Tynjala, L. Mason, & K. Lonka (Eds.), *Writing as a learning tool.* Dordrecht, Netherlands: Kluwer.

Brookhart, S. M. (2004). *Grading.* Upper Saddle River, NJ: Pearson.

Carnevale, A. P., Gainer, L. J., & Meltzer, A. S. (1988). *Workplace basics: The skills employers want.* Alexandria, VA: American Society for Training and Development.

Carr, M., & Biddlecombe, B. (1998). Metacognition in mathematics: From a constructivist perspective. In D. J. Hacker, J. Dunlosky, & A. C. Graesser (Eds.), *Metacognition in educational theory and practice.* Mahweh, NJ: Erlbaum.

Clements, D. (2000, April). Young children's ideas about geometric shapes. *Teaching Children Mathematics, 482–488.*

Cobb, P., Yackel, E., & McClain, K. (Eds.). (2000). *Symbolizing and communicating in mathematics classrooms.* Mahwah, NJ: Erlbaum.

College Board. (2004). *The New SAT 2005.* Available online at http://www.collegeboard.com/newsat/index.html.

Cramer, K. A., Post, T. A., & del Mas, R. C. (2002). Initial fraction learning by fourth and fifth grade students: A comparison of the effects of using commercial curricula with the effects of using the Rational Number Project curriculum. *Journal for Research in Mathematics Education, 33* (2), 111–144.

Curcio, R. R., & Artzt, A. F. (1998). Students communicating in small groups: Making sense of data in graphical form. In H. Steinberg, M. G. B. Bussi, & A. Sierpinska (Eds.), *Language and communication in the mathematics classroom* (pp. 179–190). Reston, VA: National Council of Teachers of Mathematics.

Davies, A. (2000). *Making classroom assessment work.* Courtenay, British Columbia, Canada: Connections.

Dewey. J. (1927). *The public and its problems.* New York: Holt.

Douville, P. (2000). Helping parents develop literacy at home. *Preventing School Failure, 44* (4), 179–183.

Driscoll, M. (1999). Fostering *algebraic thinking: A guide for teachers grades 6–10.* Portsmouth, NH: Heinemann.

Farrell, T. J. (1978). Differentiating writing from talking. *College Composition and Communication, 29,* 246–250.

Fiechtner, S. B., & Davis, E. A. (1992). Why some groups fail: A survey of students' experiences with learning groups. In A. S. Goodsell, M. R. Maher, & V. Tinto (Eds.), *Collaborative learning: A sourcebook for higher education.* Syracuse, NY: National Center on Postsecondary Teaching, Learning, & Assessment.

Flower, L., & Hayes, J. R. (1983). Uncovering cognitive processes in writing: An introduction to protocol analysis. In P. Mosenthal, L. Tamor, & S. A. Walmsley (Eds.), *Research on writing.* New York: Longman.

Fuchs, L. S., Fuchs, D., Hamlett, C. L., & Karns, K. (1998). High achieving students' interactions and performance on complex mathematical tasks as a function of homogeneous and heterogeneous pairings. *American Educational Research Journal, 35* (2), 227–267.

Fuchs, L. S., Fuchs, D., & Karns, K. (2001). Enhancing kindergartners' mathematical development: Effects of peer-assisted learning strategies. *Elementary School Journal, 101* (5), 495–510.

Fuchs, L. S., Fuchs, D., Yazdian, L., & Powell, S. R. (2002). Enhancing first-grade children's mathematical development with peer-assisted learning strategies. *School Psychology Review, 31* (4), 569–583.

Goos, M. (2002). Understanding metacognitive failure. *Journal of Mathematical Behavior, 21* (3), 283–302.

Goos, M., Galbraith, P., & Renshaw, P. (2002). Socially mediated metacognition: Creating collaborative zones of proximal development in small group problem solving. *Educational Studies in Mathematics, 49,* 193–223.

Graves, D. K. (1994). *A fresh look at writing.* Portsmouth, NH: Heinemann

Griffiths, R., & Clyne, M. (1994). Language *in the mathematics classroom: Talking, representing, recording.* Portsmouth, NH: Heinemann.

Grouws, D. A., & Cebulla, K. J. (2000). *Improving student achievement in mathematics:* Vol. 1. *Research findings.* Columbus, OH: Eric Clearinghouse (ED 463 952).

Hand, B., Prain, V., & Yore, L. (2001). Writing for learning in science. In P. Tynjak, L. Mason, & K. Lonka (Eds.), *Writing as a Learning Tool: Integrating Theory and Practice* (pp. 105–129). Dordrecht, Netherlands: Kiuwer.

Harris, M. (1979). The overgraded paper: Another case of more as less. In G. Stanford (Ed.), *Classroom practices in teaching English 1979–1980: How to handle paper load.* Urbana, IL: National Council of Teachers of English.

Hayes, J. R., & Flower, L. (1980). Identifying the organization of writing processes. In L. W. Gregg & E. W. Steinberg (Eds.), *Cognitive processes in writing* (pp. 3–30). Hillsdale, NJ: Erlbaum.

Henderson, A. T., & Mapp, K. L. (2002). *A new wave of evidence: The impact of school, family, and community connections on student achievement.* Austin, TX: Southwest Educational Development Laboratory.

Hiebert, J., Carpenter, T. P., Fennema, E., Fuson, K. C., Wearne, D., Murray, H., Olivier, A., & Human, P. (1997). *Making sense: Teaching and learning mathematics with understanding.* Portsmouth, NH: Heinemann.

Hiebert, J., & Wearne, D. (1992). Instructional tasks, classroom discourse, and students' learning in second grade arithmetic. *American Educational Research Journal, 30* (2), 393–425.

Higgins, K. M., Harris, N. A., & Kuehn, L. L. (1994). Placing assessment into the hands of young children: A study of student-generated criteria and self-assessment. *Educational Assessment, 2* (6), 309–324.

Hufferd-Ackles, K., Fuson, K. C., & Sherin, M. G. (2004). Describing levels and components of a math-talk learning community. *Journal for Research in Mathematics Education, 35* (2), 81–116.

Johnson, D., & Johnson, R. (2000). Cooperative learning methods: A meta-analysis. Available online at http://www.co-operation.org/.

Katstra, J., Tollefson, N., & Gilbert, E. (2001). The effects of peer evaluation on attitude toward writing and writing fluency of ninth grade students. *Journal of Educational Research, 80* (3), 168–172.

Kenney, P. A., & Silver, E. A. (1993). Student self-assessment in mathematics. In N. L. Webb & A. F. Coxford (Eds.), *Assessment in the mathematics classroom*. Reston, VA: National Council of Teachers of Mathematics.

Kewley, L. (1998). Peer collaboration versus teacher-directed instruction: Now two methodologies engage students in the learning process. *Journal of Research in Childhood Education, 13* (1), 27–32.

Kilpatrick, J., Swafford, J., & Findell, B. (2001). *Adding it up: Helping children learn mathematics*. Washington, DC: National Academy Press.

Koch, R., & Petterson, J. S. (2000). *The portfolio guidebook: Implementing quality in an age of standards*. Norwood, MA: Christopher-Gordon.

Kramarski, B., Mevarch, Z. R., & Arami, M. (2002). The effects of metacognitive instruction on solving mathematical authentic tasks. *Educational Studies in Mathematics, 49,* 225–250.

Kramarski, B., & Ritkof, R. (2002). The effects of metacognition and email interactions on learning graphing. *Journal of Computer Assisted Learning, 18,* 33–43.

Krulik, S., & Rudnick, J. A. (1999). Innovative tasks to improve critical- and creative-thinking skills. In L. V. Stiff & F. R. Curcio (Eds.), *Developing mathematical reasoning in grades K–12* (pp. 138–145). Reston, VA: National Council of Teachers of Mathematics.

Kuhn, D., Shaw, V., & Felton, M. (1997). Effects of didactic interaction on argumentative reasoning. *Cognition and Instruction, 15* (3), 287–315.

Kulm, G. (Ed.) (1990). New directions for mathematics assessment. In *Assessing higher order thinking in mathematics* (pp. 71–78). Washington, DC: American Association for the Advancement of Science.

Lester, F. K. (1989). The role of metacognition in mathematical problem solving: A study of two grade seven classes (Report No. 85-50346). Washington, DC: National Science Foundation.

Lim, L. (2004, March). Implementing journal writing in grade 9 applied mathematics. *Ontario Mathematics Gazette, 42* (4), 14–18.

Linchevski, L., & Kutscher, B. (1998). Tell me with whom you're learning and I'll tell you how much you've learned: Mixed-ability versus same-ability grouping in mathematics. *Journal for Research in Mathematics Education, 29* (5), 533–554.

Lindquist, M. M., & Elliott, P. C. (1996). Communication—An imperative for change. In P. C. Elliott & M. J. Kenney (Eds.), *Communication in mathematics, K–12 and beyond* (pp. 1–10). Reston, VA: National Council of Teachers of Mathematics.

Linnakyla, P. (2001). Portfolio: Integrating writing, learning and assessment. In P. Tynjala, L. Mason, & K. Lonka (Eds.), *Writing as a learning tool* (pp. 145–160). Dordrecht, Netherlands: Kluwer.

Martinez, J.G.R., & Martinez, N. C. (2000, January). Teaching math with stories. *Teaching K–8, 54–56.*

Marzano, Robert J. (2000). A *new era of school reform: Going where the research takes us.* Aurora, CO: Mid-Continent Research for Education and Learning. Available online at http://www.mcrel.org.

Mathematical Sciences Education Board. (1993). *Measuring what counts: A policy brief.* Washington, DC: National Academy Press.

McDonald, B., & Boud, D. (2003). The impact of self-assessment on achievement: The effects of self-assessment training on performance in external examinations. *Assessment in Education, 10* (2), 209–220.

McNair, R. E. (1998). Building a context for mathematical discussion. In M. Lampert & M. L. Blunk (Eds.), *Talking mathematics in school: Studies of teaching and learning* (pp. 82–106). Cambridge, UK: Cambridge University Press.

Meaney, T. (2002). *Does speaking improve students' writing in mathematics?* Paper presented at the Annual Conference of the Australian Association for Research in Education, Brisbane, Australia.

Meier, J., & Rishel, T. (1998). Writing *in the teaching and learning of mathematics.* Washington, DC: Mathematical Association of America.

Middleton, J. A., & Goepfert, P. (1996). Inventive *strategies for teaching mathematics.* Washington, DC: American Psychological Association.

Moffett, J. (1981). *Coming on center.* Montclair, NJ: Boyton/Cook.

Moffett, J., & Wagner, B. J. (1992). *Student-centered language arts, K–12.* Portsmouth, NH: Heinemann.

Morgan, C. (1998). *Writing mathematically: The discourse of investigation.* London: Falmer Press.

Nagel, G. K. (2001). Effective *grouping for literacy instruction.* Boston: Allyn & Bacon.

National Assessment Governing Board. (1998). *Writing framework and specifications for the 1998 national assessment of educational progress.* Washington, DC: U.S. Department of Education. Available online at http://www.nagb.org.

National Center for Education Statistics. (2004). *2003 mathematics and reading assessment results.* Washington, DC: U.S. Department of Education. Available online at http://nces.ed.gov/nationsreportcard/.

National Council of Teachers of Mathematics (NCTM). (1991). *Professional standards for teaching mathematics.* Reston, VA: Author.

National Council of Teachers of Mathematics (NCTM). (1995). *Assessment standards for school mathematics.* Reston, VA: Author.

National Council of Teachers of Mathematics (NCTM). (2000). *Principles and standards for school mathematics.* Reston, VA: Author.

National Research Council. (2001). *Adding it up: Helping children learn mathematics.* Washington, DC: Author.

Nitko, A. J. (2001). *Educational assessment of students.* Columbus, OH: Merrill-Prentice Hall.

Northwest Regional Educational Laboratory. *6+1 trait writing.* Available online at http://www.nwrel.org/assessment/.

O'Connor, M. C. (1998). Language socialization in the mathematics classroom: Discourse practices and mathematical thinking. In M. Lampert & M. L. Bunk (Eds.), *Talking mathematics in school: Studies of teaching and learning* (pp. 17–55). Cambridge, UK: Cambridge University Press.

Oladunni, M. O. (1998). An experimental study on the effectiveness of metacognitive and heuristic problem solving techniques on computational performance of students in mathematics. *International Journal of Mathematics Education in Science and Technology, 29* (6), 867–874.

Pandey, T. (1990). *Authentic mathematics assessment.* Washington, DC: ERIC Clearinghouse (ED 354 245).

Paris, S. G., & Paris, A. H. (2001). Classroom applications of research on self-regulated learning. *Educational Psychologist, 36* (2), 89–101.

Park, O. (1984). Example comparison strategy versus attribute identification strategy in concept learning. *American Educational Research Journal, 21,* 145–162.

Polya, G. (1957). How *to solve it?* Princeton, NJ: Princeton University Press.

Powell, A. B. (1997). Capturing, examining, and responding to mathematical thinking through writing. *The Clearing House, 71* (1), 21–25.

Pugalee, D. K. (1998). Promoting mathematical learning through writing. *Mathematics in School, 27* (1), 19–22.

Pugalee, D. K. (1999). Constructing a model of mathematical literacy. *Clearing House, 73* (1), 19–22.

Pugalee, D. K. (2001a). Using communication to develop students' mathematical literacy. *Mathematics Teaching in the Middle School, 6* (5), 296–299.

Pugalee, D. K. (2001b). Writing, mathematics, and metacognition: Looking for connections through students' work in mathematical problem solving. *School Science and Mathematics, 101* (5), 236–245.

Pugalee, D. K. (2004). A comparison of verbal and written descriptions of students' problem solving processes. *Educational Studies in Mathematics, 55,* 27–47.

Pugalee, D. K., Bissell, B., Lock, C., & Douville, P. (2003). The treatment of mathematical communication in mainstream algebra texts. *Proceedings of the mathematics Into the 21st century conference* (pp. 238–241). Brno, Czechoslovakia: Mathematics Into the 21st Century Project.

Pugalee, D. K., Douville, P., Lock, C. R., & Wallace, J. (2002, August). Authentic tasks and mathematical problem solving. *Proceedings of the mathematics into the 21st century conference* (pp. 303–306). Palermo, Sicily: Mathematics Into the 21st Century Project.

Rivard, L. P., & Straw, S. B. (2000). The effect of talk and writing on learning science: An exploratory study. *Science Education, 84* (5), 566–593.

Rudnitsky, A., Etheredge, S., Freeman, S.J.M., & Gilbert, T. (1995). Learning to solve addition and subtraction word problems through structure-plus-writing approach. *Journal for Research in Mathematics Education, 26* (5), 467–486.

Senk, S. L., & Thompson, D. R. (Eds.). (2002). *Standards-based school mathematics curricula: What are they? What do students learn?* Mahwah, NJ: Erlbaum.

Sexton, R., & Ballew, H. (1988, March). *Research videos on problem solving.* Paper presented at the North Carolina Council of Teachers of Mathematics Eastern Regional Conference, Raleigh.

Silver, E. A., & Stein, M. K. (1996). The QUASAR project: The "revolution of the possible" in mathematics instruction reform in urban middle schools. *Urban Education, 30* (4), 476–521.

Slavin, R. E. (1995). *Cooperative learning: Theory, research, and* practice (2nd ed.). Boston: Allyn & Bacon.

Slavin, R. E. (1996). Research for the future: Research on cooperative learning and achievement—what we know, what we need to know. *Contemporary Educational Psychology, 21* (1), 43–69.

Stacey, K., & Gooding, A. (1998). Communication and learning in small-group discussions. In Steinbring, H., Bussi, M. G., & Sierpinska, A. (Eds.), *Language and communication in the mathematics classroom* (pp. 191–206). Reston, VA: National Council of Teachers of Mathematics.

Steinbring, H., Bussi, M. G., & Sierpinska, A. (Eds.). (1998). *Language and communication in the mathematics classroom.* Reston, VA: National Council of Teachers of Mathematics.

Stepanek, J. (2000). *Mathematics and science classrooms: Building a community of learners.* Portland, OR: Northwest Regional Educational Laboratory.

Tennyson, R. D., & Park, O. C. (1980). The teaching of concepts: A review of instructional design literature. *Review of Educational Research, 50* (1), 55–70.

Tompkins, G. E. (2003). *Literacy for the 21st century* (3rd ed.). Upper Saddle River, NJ: Merrill/Prentice-Hall.

Turner, J. C., et al. (2002). The classroom environment and students' reports of avoidance strategies in mathematics: A multimedia study. *Journal of Educational Psychology, 94* (1), 88–106.

Tynjala, P., Mason, L., & Lonka, K. (Eds.). (2001). *Writing as a learning tool: An introduction.* In *Writing as a learning tool.* Dordrecht, Netherlands: Kluwer.

Vygotsky, L. S. (1987). Thinking and speech. In R. W. Rieber & A. S. Carton (Eds.), *The collected works of L. S. Vygotsky* (pp. 39–243). New York: Plenum Press.

Webb, N. M. (1991). Task-related verbal interaction and mathematics learning in small groups. *Journal for Research in Mathematics Education, 22,* 366–389.

Webnox. (2003). *Hyperdictionary.* Available online at http://www.hyperdictionary.com.

Winograd, K. (1992). What fifth graders learn when they write their own math problems. *Educational Leadership, 64* (4), 64–66.

Wiltse, E. M. (2002, Summer). Correlates of college students' use of instructors' comments. *Journalism & Mass Communication Educator,* 126–138.

Wood, T. (1998). Alternative patterns of communication in mathematics classes: Funneling or focusing? In H. Steinbring, M. G. Bussi, & A. Sierpinska (Eds.), *Language and communication in the mathematics classroom* (pp. 167–178). Reston, VA: National Council of Teachers of Mathematics.

Yackel, E. (2000, August). *Creating a mathematics classroom environment that fosters the development of mathematical argumentation.* Paper presented at the Ninth International Congress of Mathematical Education, Tokyo.

Index

About the Author

David Pugalee is Associate Professor of Education at the University of North Carolina Charlotte where he is coordinator of the Ph.D. program in Curriculum and Instruction. He earned a Ph.D. in mathematics education from the University of North Carolina at Chapel Hill. He has a bachelors degree in psychology and masters degrees in mathematics and curriculum supervision. His teaching experience includes teaching mathematics at the elementary, middle and secondary levels before moving  into higher education. He has an extensive list of publications including research articles in *Educational Studies in Mathematics* and *School Science and Mathematics*. His works also include several books including lead author for several in the middle grades *Navigations* series published by the National Council of Teachers of Mathematics. His research interest is mathematical literacy—the relationship between language and mathematics learning.